Country Walks
from Bath

COUNTRY WALKS
FROM BATH

Andrew Swift

AKEMAN PRESS

Published by AKEMAN PRESS
www.akemanpress.com

© Andrew Swift 2017

ISBN 978-0-9933988-1-0

Front cover: Looking west over Englishcombe from Twerton Round Hill
Back cover: Looking west from Lansdown
Facing title page: Looking across the Woolley Valley to Little Solsbury

Printed in the UK by the Pureprint Group

FSC
www.fsc.org
MIX
Paper from
responsible sources
FSC® C022913

Contents

Extra Features

Introduction

This collection of walks is a sequel to those in *On Foot in Bath*, but, whereas the focus in that book was on the city, the focus here is on the surrounding countryside. As in *On Foot*, however, all the walks start in the city centre, and all – except for the last two, which entail catching a bus or train back to Bath – end there as well.

Of all the things that make such Bath an inspiring place to live or to visit, one of the most important – its setting amid countryside of unparalleled beauty and variety – is frequently overlooked. The green hills that encircle the city are a constant backdrop to the bustle of its streets, and offer a ready means of escape from their fumes and frivolity. The architect John Wood, who designed some of Bath's most iconic buildings, was well aware of this. 'The difficulty of ascending our hills is not so great as is generally reported,' he wrote, 'but when surmounted, what beautiful prospects do they give? ... I will venture to say, that ... so many beautiful points of view, and matters of curiosity may be found about Bath, as conducive to the health and pleasure of mankind in general, as can be met with in ten times the space of ground in any other country.'

Remarkably, over 250 years later the integrity of Bath's rural setting remains largely intact. When Bath was accorded World Heritage status in 1987, it was the whole of the city, not just its major buildings, that was included – recognition that the city's setting was at least as important as its buildings.

The 14 walks in this book offer a chance to reconnect with what, for many 18th-century visitors, was the city's main attraction. Walking in the countryside around Bath has an illustrious tradition. It not only formed part of the city's much-vaunted health cure, but also enabled visitors to commune with the ideal of rural bliss extolled by the writers and artists who moulded 18th taste.

No one was more adept at evoking that pastoral idyll than Thomas Gainsborough, who came to Bath to work as a portrait painter, but escaped when he could to the hills around the city. There he would sketch the 'cicumjacent scenery', which, according to his friend Ozias Humphry, he regarded as 'in many parts, picturesque, and beautiful to a high Degree'.

Another painter who loved Bath was Benjamin West. In 1807, shortly after he had been re-elected president of the Royal Academy for a second term, he 'spoke of Bath and its vicinity with rapture as abounding with picturesque scenery. Take Bath & 20 miles round it he said, and there is not in the world anything superior to it. Rocks of the finest forms for a painter ... quarries worked out, now most picturesque and romantic ... distances the most beautiful, roads with occasional pools & streams of water falling from the hills ... Take Tivoli away and Rome and its vicinity of 20 miles [is] not to be compared with Bath & its neighbourhood.'

West was not alone in regarding the scenery around Bath as incomparable, and the survival of so much that delighted 18th and 19th century visitors makes the city a matchless walking centre today. And, bearing in mind that Bath in its Georgian heyday was a winter resort, it is very much a walking centre that can be enjoyed all year round. Although the footpaths are more likely to be muddy in winter, with the trees bare of leaves, the prospects – to use a good 18th century term – are largely unimpeded, and winter sunsets have a magic all their own. As Edmund Rack wrote in 1780, 'even in the nakedness of winter our prospects are pleasing. The wild irregularity of surface, the extent of varied country, the numbers of objects, and the changes of scene at every step furnishes the spectator with unabated pleasure. Dull indeed must be the soul whose Hours can hang heavy on his Hands at Bath.'

It is not just the scenery that makes the countryside around Bath so fascinating. The awareness that you are treading where countless generations have left their mark is inescapable. These 14 walks are walks through history, be that in the form of iron age hillforts, Civil War battlefields, lost pleasure gardens or abandoned towpaths. Ancient holloways and green lanes wind through woods to hamlets lost amid the fields, to gabled manors, tiny churches, huddled farms and country pubs. Further afield lie villages such as Freshford, Kelston and Saltford, and the historic weaving towns of Corsham and Bradford on Avon, while to the north, high on Cotswold edge, sits Marshfield, once one of the most prosperous towns in Gloucestershire, but now, as if frozen in time, a place that history has passed by.

The countryside around Bath was also a cradle of early industry. Canals, tramways and inclined planes were built to carry stone from quarries high in the hills. Railways were driven through quiet valleys, competing for traffic from the burgeoning Somerset coalfield. Mills powered by fast-flowing brooks turned wool to cloth, the main source of the area's prosperity for centuries. Of all this activity, nothing now remains but ruins and reminders.

Such is the terrain which these walks explore. They can be no more than an introduction to the riches it has to offer, but if they encourage more people to seek out those riches, and rediscover the health and recreational benefits Bath's unique setting has to offer, they will have achieved their aim.

A FEW PRACTICALITIES

All the walks start in Kingston Parade, the square south of Bath Abbey, and all (with the exception of the last two) also end there. As for the last two walks – Walk 13 ends at Corsham, which has a frequent bus service to Bath, while Walk 14 ends at Bradford on Avon, which has a frequent train service to Bath.

Walks 1 to 4 are an introduction to the countryside on the city's doorstep. Walk 1 visits a series of viewpoints – some well-known, some unfamiliar – along the southern escarpment. Walks 2 to 4, each about four miles long, explore pockets of countryside within the city.

The remainder of the walks are longer – ranging from 10 to 17 miles – but in every case shorter options are available. These generally entail using public transport at the beginning or end of the walk to get to or from the city's outer limits. These options are described in the text and indicated on route maps at the start of each walk, which also show the distance (in miles) between intermediate points.

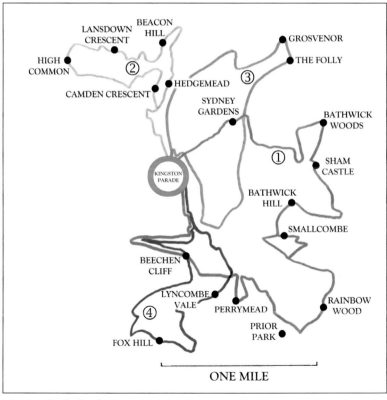

Routes of walks 1 to 4

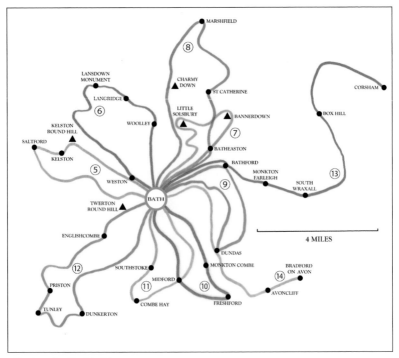

Routes of walks 5 to 14

Symbols used on the route maps are:

Points from which buses can be caught to or from the city centre

Railway stations

Pubs

The route maps are not intended as navigational aids. A detailed map is all but essential on all except the first four walks. Although I have endeavoured to make the directions as clear and unambiguous as possible, one wrong turning can, as I have found from experience, lead you badly astray. Using maps may not prevent this, but they are invaluable in working out where you went wrong. Another consideration is that things referred to in the text may change: stiles may be replaced by gates, fences built, hedgerows grubbed up, footpaths rerouted, waymarks removed. Such impediments cannot be avoided by the use of maps, but maps can help you get round them; without maps you can be very much at sea.

Ordnance Survey (OS) Explorer Maps, at a scale of 1:25 000 (2½ inches to a mile) are recommended. OS Explorer 155 covers the routes of walks 1-9, but for walks 10-14 needs to be supplemented by OS Explorer 142 or 156. However, AA Walker's Map 25, which is based on the OS maps, covers the routes of all the walks, except No 13, where it needs to be supplemented by OS Explorer 156.

For ease of navigation, directions in the text appear in ***bold italic type***.

I have not indicated how long each walk is likely to take, as this will depend not only on how fast you walk but also on how long you take to look at things en route. Generally, though, if you walk at a reasonable pace with occasional stops, you should cover around two miles an hour. Walking briskly with few or no stops should enable you to cover around three miles an hour.

Information on pubs and cafés is given for guidance only, and, as it is liable to change, you are advised to check before setting out. As it is unlikely you will be calling in for an evening meal while on a country walk, I have only indicated when food is served during the day. Also, although it is unlikely you will turn up at a pub before it opens, 'open all day' should be taken to mean from around 11am or noon.

Although walking in the country should be a pleasure, there are certain rules to follow. If a gate is closed when you come to it, ensure you close it behind you. Leave no litter. Light no fires. If you have a dog, keep it under close control, especially near livestock. Sheep and cattle are likely to be encountered on all the longer walks, and, while the only thing you should have to worry about with sheep is ensuring your dog is on a lead, with cattle the situation is trickier.

In 2013, a man was trampled to death by cows while walking his dog along a footpath near the Kennet & Avon Canal at Winsley. After his death, it transpired that at least three other people had been injured in similar incidents in the same area in the previous five years. This footpath, needless to say, does not feature in this book of walks. I have also routed walks away from fields with cows where I considered there to be any element of risk. Nevertheless, cows will be encountered, not least on National Trust land around Bath. While it is extremely unlikely you will experience any problems, the advice, if you do, is to move as quickly and quietly as possible (but without running), avoid getting between cows and their calves, and, if necessary, let your dog off the lead so he or she can get out of trouble.

Finally, wear robust footwear, preferably walking boots, and make sure you carry plenty of water – as well as something to snack on. Climbing hills, especially in warm weather, is thirsty work, and on some of the walks there is nowhere to stop for refreshment.

Setting the Scene: Walk 1
Along the Southern Escarpment

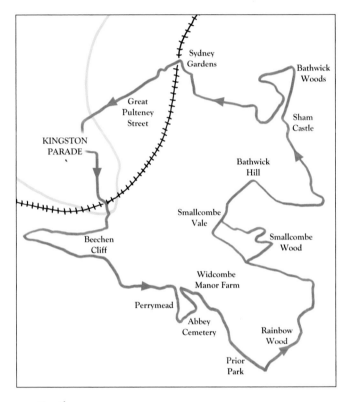

Distance: 7 miles

Terrain: Some steep and muddy paths, as well as rough field tracks, steep steps and a couple of stiles. There are usually horses in the field beyond Beechen Cliff, as well as cows on National Trust land at certain times of year.

Pubs and cafés: None en route.

Map: OS Explorer 155 or AA Walker's Map 25 (although not all footpaths are shown).

Opposite: Looking north-westward from Smallcombe to Kelston Round Hill

This walk follows the escarpment on the south side of Bath, taking in as many different views of the city as possible. The most striking feature of many of the views is the contrast between the busy city and the quiet, secluded spots which look down upon it. Each comes as a revelation, giving a new angle on the city, with its topography and buildings rearranged, some features now prominent, some hidden, but always creating a fascinating if occasionally bewildering whole. Although some of the walk is along quiet roads, much of it is through woods and fields, thanks largely to the National Trust, which is one of the major landowners in the city.

Starting in the city centre, the walk heads up to Beechen Cliff for the most celebrated prospect of Bath. From there it heads for the gentler charms of Perrymead and a view of the city framed by crumbling Victorian tombs. Then it is on through old Widcombe and past Prior Park for a distant view of the city with Pulteney Bridge at its heart. From there, we head down Widcombe Hill to Smallcombe Vale – and a chance to visit a tract of ancient woodland – before walking up through Bathwick Fields for one of the classic views of the city. After climbing to Sham Castle, a woodland path past old quarry workings leads to the grand climax of the walk – a surprisingly little-known view taking in the whole sweep of the Avon valley, from Twerton Round Hill in the west to Little Solsbury in the east, with Bath at its centre. Finally, we drop down to Sydney Gardens for a final – and rather unexpected – urban panorama, before heading back to the city centre.

Starting in Kingston Parade, head east along York Street. Turn right at the end, bear left along North Parade and right along Pierrepont Street. Continue along Manvers Street and at the end go through a tunnel to the left of the railway station. Carry on across a footbridge over the river, cross the two sets of pedestrian lights ahead, bear right for a few metres, and turn left up Lyncombe Hill.

Take the first right along Calton Road. As you climb, you will get glimpses of the city between the buildings. Carry on, with the woods of Beechen Cliff above you and the tower of St Mark's church below. Continue past modern terraces, with views down flights of steps of the city below. These terraces replaced rows of 19th-century houses which were demolished in the 1960s, although some had already fallen victim to wartime bombing. There were houses on the left as well, and you can still see remnants of their walls amidst the undergrowth.[1]

At the end, carry on along a path, cross a road and carry on uphill. This is Holloway, now a quiet cul de sac, but for centuries the main

---

1 More on the lost houses below Beechen Cliff, along with old maps, can be found in Walk 15 in *On Foot in Bath*

road into Bath from the south. Opposite Paradise House, you will see a gateway and steps which led to a house destroyed by bombing in 1942. A little further up is the chapel of St Mary Magdalen, founded around 1100.

Cross and go up steps beside the horse trough opposite. Follow a path as it curves up steps past the entrance to Magdalen Gardens, a tiny municipal park opened in July 1902 and recently restored by volunteers after years of neglect. *After climbing more steps, the path bears left along the escarpment* – still climbing steeply – with houses on the right and views so fine that in the 1920s Cedric Chivers, the Mayor of Bath, presented a toposcope so that visitors could identify

The Chapel of St Mary Magdalen seen through the boughs of the ancient Judas Tree that stands beside it

prominent buildings and landmarks. Today, the view is somewhat less extensive, as many of the landmarks are hidden by trees, while many of the buildings have been lost to bombing or post-war redevelopment.

Victorian photographs of Beechen Cliff – such as the one below – show that, despite its name, its slopes were largely bare. In the early twentieth century, the council decided to plant pines and rhododendrons emulating those in the chines at Bournemouth. A century on, the legacy

of those plantings, and of unchecked growth, means that the views which could once be enjoyed from Beechen Cliff have dwindled to a few tree-fringed vistas – magnificent, to be sure, but also very frustrating, when you consider what has been lost.

As you carry on, you come to Alexandra Park, named in honour of Edward VII's queen in 1902. There is a glimpse of St Mark's below, with Southgate and the railway station beyond. Then, as the view opens up ahead to Bathwick Hill, you come to a bench with a classic urban panorama – the curve of the river bisected by the curve of the railway and the city's streets extending to the tree-capped hills in the distance. Far below – as a measure of how far you have climbed – are the traffic lights where you crossed earlier.

Carry on as the path starts heading downhill (watching out for cunningly placed trip steps). At the end of the allotments, when you come to a kissing gate (KG) on the right, go through it. There are two tracks here – take the one on the left heading diagonally across to the far corner of the field. Carry on in the same direction through another field, where there may be horses.

Go through a gate at the end and turn left down a road. When you come to a crossroads, carry straight on down Rosemount Lane (once known as Rough Hill) which leads steeply downhill to the valley of the Lyn Brook. Over to your right, behind the houses of Perrymead, is the pyramidal spire of the Abbey Cemetery's mortuary chapel. As you continue downhill, you also have a good view, to the left, of the Colosseum-like curve of Widcombe Crescent.

At the main road, turn right and, after a few metres, turn right again up Perrymead. After 250m, you will see the lodge and gateway

The view from Perrymead

of a 19th-century mansion called The Cloisters. To the right, beyond Hillcrest, is Perrymead Court, once home to Venanzio Rauzzini, an Italian castrato, composer and impresario, who, after a glittering European career, settled in Bath around 1781. When Joseph Haydn visited London in 1794, he travelled down to Bath to visit Rauzzini and spent several days here. A watercolour by William Capon of the view from Rauzzini's garden, which was considered one of the finest in Bath, is in the Victoria Art Gallery.

Turn left uphill past The Cloisters and after 40m go through a KG on the left into the Abbey Cemetery (ST758635). *Follow a rough path past the chapel*, which commands a distant view of the city framed by the mournful serenity of the 19th-century cemetery. The Abbey Cemetery opened in 1844, and was designed by John Claudius Loudon, who had published an influential treatise 'On the Laying Out, Planting, and Managing of Cemeteries, and on the Improvement of Churchyards' the previous year. Loudon summed up his philosophy thus:

> The main object of a burial-ground is the disposal of the remains of the dead in such a manner as that their decomposition, and return to the earth from which they sprung, shall not prove injurious to the living; either by affecting their health, or shocking their feelings, opinions, or prejudices. A secondary object is, or ought to be, the improvement of the moral sentiments and general taste of all classes, and more especially of the great masses of society.

Before it opened, burials had taken place in the abbey, a practice which was roundly condemned by Philip Thicknesse in 1778:

> The vast number of bodies buried within the church and near the surface, and the frequency of the ground being opened, before the effect of the putrefaction is over, the doors and windows not being sufficiently, or constantly kept open, renders the confined air perceptibly disagreeable at first entering the church; and, we are told, there is an opening, or ventilator, in the roof, over which if any one place their nose, they will meet, at all times, a stench scarce to be imagined. The malignant sore throat is not very uncommon in Bath, and who can say from what source of corruption it arises?

Loudon's replacement of what was effectively a charnel house with landscaped grounds, in which architecturally uplifting monuments stood amidst ornamental trees and shrubs, was hugely influential, and has bequeathed to us a legacy of green spaces and wildlife habitats in our towns and cities. The Abbey Cemetery may have been one of the first garden cemeteries, but, given its setting and the vision of its creator, it remains one of the most inspiring.

As you *follow the main path, curving left downhill beside a wall*, to your right you will see the 15th-century church of St Thomas à Becket,

5

with Widcombe House beside it and Crowe Hall above. Over to your left, meanwhile, is the wooded profile of Beechen Cliff. *Continue down the path and go through the gates at the end.*

Cross the main road and turn down Church Street. After 120m, just past the entrance to Little Orchard, turn right along a footpath beside a noisy brook. After the path curves left, you can glimpse, in the grounds of Widcombe Manor Farm, an octagonal dovecote with more than a passing resemblance to the Tower of the Winds in Athens.

The view from the Abbey Cemetery of Crowe Hall high above the church of St Thomas à Becket and Widcombe House

The view of the city with Pulteney Bridge and weir at its heart

After climbing steps, turn right along a lane, and follow it as it curves past the gates of Prior Park Gardens. At the end, turn left and go up a path to the right of a KG (ST761634). *After going through a metal squeeze stile, bear slightly left to follow a faint track heading up a field, and carry on in the same direction.* At the top of the field, turn to take in a view of the city, framed by the wooded hills of Widcombe, with Pulteney Bridge and weir at its heart.

As you continue, you will see two KGs ahead. Go through the one on the right and, as you head towards another KG, you will see the Abbey Cemetery over to your right.

After going through the KG, bear left between gateposts to follow a path beside a fence. As the views open up eastwards, you can see Rainbow Wood House ahead. When you reach its private drive, follow steps up to the right. At the top, bear left alongside a hedge and follow it as it curves right. When you reach a stony path, turn left through a gateway by a Lyncombe & Widcombe (L&W) boundary stone.

After another 170m, when the path curves right, go through a KG on the left to follow an old drungway[1] between stone walls (ST767638). *Carry on as it drops steeply downhill through woods to emerge on a busy road.* This is Widcombe Hill, and on your left, by Macaulay Buildings, is another entrance to Rainbow Wood House. *Cross the road to a turnpike trust boundary marker and*, as you *turn left downhill*, a very different panorama of the city opens up. Over to your right, 19th-century villas on Bathwick Hill can be seen amidst the trees. Prominent among them is Bathwick Grange, originally known as Montebello, which Henry Goodridge, the architect of Beckford's Tower and Cleveland Place, built for himself. Its Italianate campanile rises above a tower which, like the dovecote at Widcombe Manor Farm, recalls the Tower of the Winds in Athens.

Bathwick Grange

1 The local name for a narrow path, generally between two walls. Although its use seems to be confined to Bath and north east Somerset, similar paths are known as drangs in Devon and Cornwall, and as drongs in Dorset. According to the *Oxford English Dictionary*, it derives from the Old English word 'dring', meaning 'to press or compress', which has an etymological link with 'throng'.

After 150m, go through a KG into Smallcombe Vale. Here you have a choice – a straightforward option, entailing a walk across a field and down steps, or a more challenging alternative down a steep and muddy woodland path, which may entail negotiating fallen trees.

● *For the easier option, turn left immediately through another KG. Follow a track straight ahead, heading for the Abbey and Kelston Round Hill on the horizon. At the end of the field, go through a KG in the far right-hand corner and follow a track heading steeply down steps to Smallcombe Vale* (ST761642). *Cross a lane at the bottom, carry on up the footpath opposite, skip the next four paragraphs and pick the directions up again at* ●.

● *For the more adventurous option, follow a track diagonally across the field to the right, go through a handgate into Smallcombe Wood and follow the track straight ahead.* This is believed to be the only surviving tract of ancient woodland in Bath. Evidence of the trees that were coppiced here over 250 years ago comes from the *Bath Chronicle* for 6 March 1766, which carried a notice to the effect

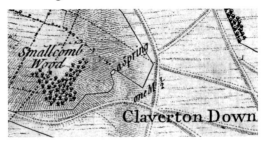

Smallcombe Wood on Thorpe's map of 1742

that 'some malicious and evil-disposed Person or Persons have lately committed divers Trespasses and Misdemeanors within the Manor of Bathwicke, belonging to the Hon Gen Pulteney, by cutting down and carrying away Poles of Oak, Ash, &c, growing in the Wood called Smallcombe Wood' and offering a reward of two guineas to anyone who could bring the perpetrators to justice. In the mid-19th century, there were several convictions for stealing wood from Smallcombe, and, although the type of wood was not always specified, when it was, it was generally hazel.

Carry straight on and, after 250m, when the track forks, bear left. The going is not only muddy here, but also slippery, and, although rough steps have been provided, you may have to negotiate fallen trees. However, as you continue on down alongside a spring, you come to a magical spot where small-leaved limes have fallen across the spring and sent up new shoots, to create an extraordinary display of rejuvenation and resilience. Small-leaved limes were once common. Indeed, analysis of pollen deposits indicates that, 5,000 years ago, they were the dominant trees in England's Wildwood. Today, however, they are largely confined to ancient woodland, which makes this arboreal spectacle all the more memorable.

At the bottom, bear left alongside the fence to follow the track as it winds through the woods – although you may first want to divert to the right, crossing a couple of springs, to take in what must surely be the most unusual view of the city. Framed by Smallcombe Vale and looking due west, the only instantly recognisable landmarks are the spire of St John's Roman Catholic church and the Western Riverside development beyond. For the rest, it hardly looks like Bath at all.

Smallcombe Wood carpeted with wild garlic in early spring

Bathwick Cemetery in the early 20th century with Smallcombe Wood beyond

After following the track through the woods for 150m, you come to a fork. Do not take the steps heading up to the left, but carry straight on, and after going down a few rough steps, continue through a gap in the wall of Smallcombe Cemetery. Opened in 1856, its mortuary chapel was designed by Thomas Fuller, who also designed Bath's Newark Works and the Canadian Parliament Buildings in Ottawa (ST765642). *Head down past the chapel, go through the gates and head along a lane for 150m, before turning right up a footpath.*

● *Follow the path as it winds steeply uphill, and, after going through a KG, carry on along a well-trodden track as it curves right through a gap in a hedge to a KG in the top corner of the next field,* where there is a seat to take in a superb view of the city.

From here, head up to the road and turn right. The next part of the walk, up Bathwick Hill, is the least scenic – and most frustrating. Least scenic because views to the right over Smallcombe Vale are hidden, apart from fugitive glimpses, by high walls; most frustrating because, although there is a succession of supremely elegant Italianate villas on the left, they are largely hidden behind trees and shrubs. Just after passing Woodside Nursing Home on the right, however, you can look up to the left to see the tower of Bathwick Grange which you saw earlier from across the valley.

After 550m, turn left up North Lane, cross the road at the top and turn left. After crossing the entrance to the university campus, turn right along a bridleway. When it forks, bear left up a stepped path past a quarry face. When you come to a footbridge on the right, bear left across a slab stile and follow a track alongside the fence on the right. At the end, turn right, across a stile, to Sham Castle, aptly

Sham Castle

10

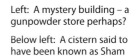

Left: A mystery building – a gunpowder store perhaps?

Below left: A cistern said to have been known as Sham Castle Holy Well

Below: A waterworks stone

named, for the structure that looks so imposing from afar is found to be no more than a sham by those who take the trouble to walk up here. It does, however, command a magnificent view of the city framed by trees – or, if you step through to the back of the castle, by a gothic arch. The marker stone you can see below the castle was connected with Bathwick Water Works, established in the 18th century to convey water from the springs on the hillside to houses in the valley below.

Bear left, following a rough path down past a small stone structure, which, if you look inside, you will discover has a vaulted roof. This suggests it was used to store gunpowder for use in nearby quarries, as the vault would have absorbed some of the impact in the event of an accidental explosion.

After crossing a drive, once again you have a choice:

● *For a shorter walk (which misses what is arguably the finest panorama of the city), go through the KG ahead, head straight downhill and go through a KG at the bottom* (ST764649). *After walking down a few steps, cross the road with care – and skip the next six paragraphs, picking the directions up again at* ●.

● *For a longer walk through woods and fields (parts of which are liable to be muddy after rain), turn right alongside the fence and go down a flight of steps.* After passing another waterworks stone, you come to a spring flowing into a basin, with another marker stone in the

11

undergrowth behind it. Apparently, this was once known as Sham Castle Holy Well.[1] Carry on as the path curves through Bathwick Woods, where there is evidence of extensive quarrying, some of it dating back to Roman times. *When you come to a KG, go through it and carry on until you come to a broad track*, down which carts carried stone from the quarries. On the far side of the track is a seat commanding a view across the valley (ST765653).

Turn left down the track, and, just before it emerges into the open, look to the left to see a small stone structure, masked by a tightly packed stand of ash. In high summer, it may be totally hidden, but, if you turn off the path, its location should be revealed by the tell-tale sound of rushing water. This is the entrance to one of the underground reservoirs hidden beneath these grassy slopes. All around, the ground is littered with moss-covered branches, tangled with roots and brambles and muddied with rivulets and puddles, in a rough approximation of what those wandering this hillside would have come upon millennia ago, when the hot springs in the valley below flowed untroubled into the Avon. As you carry on down the track, look to your right to see long lines of terraces, up to two metres high, running along the contours. It has been suggested that these may have been building platforms, connected in some way with the nearby quarries.[2]

A rough approximation of what those wandering this hillside would have come upon millennia ago

1 Quinn, *Holy Wells*, 104-5
2 An Archaeological and Historic Landscape Survey of the National Trust Bath Skyline Properties, Bath Archaeological Trust, 2003

Carry on as the track curves downhill. Just before you reach a gate at the bottom leading onto a road, you will see a spring issuing into a basin on the left. Turn left beside it and double back uphill, heading diagonally towards the wood line you can see at the very top of the large field. There are no footpaths here, and the going can be rough, but this all belongs to the National Trust, which you can thank once again for preserving access to such a spectacularly situated – and so little frequented – tract of land.

When you reach the top of the field, turn to take in an almost uninterrupted view of the city laid out below you. Although the course of the railway can be seen – as it could from Beechen Cliff – the river is hidden from view. Its course, however, can be made out by tracing the line of buildings that follow it through the city. It is not just Bath that is seen to best advantage from here; this is also the best place to appreciate the full sweep of the hills girdling the city to the north and west. To the left, high above the spire of St John's Roman Catholic church, is the Silbury-like profile of Twerton Round Hill. Beyond the Abbey are the tree-capped hills above Newton St Loe, to the north of which the high ground above Keynsham stands silhouetted against the sky. Further north, beyond the asymmetrical curve of Camden Crescent, is Kelston Round Hill. Eastward, beyond the Swainswick valley, lies Charmy Down, and, as you continue along the top of the field and look back, you will see Little Solsbury just visible beyond the edge of Bathwick Woods.

A winter sunset, from the slopes below Bathwick Woods

13

Looking eastward over Larkhall

As you carry on with the woods on your left, you will notice, a little way down the field, a small plot of more or less level ground, which appears to have been created by building up the earth to make a platform. The chances are, if it was man-made, that it was connected with quarrying operations in the woods above, but how tempting it is to imagine that some sort of building once stood here – a farmstead or villa, say – and to think of the view it would have had.

Carry on round the edge of the field, before heading through a well-defined gap into a smaller field, where you will see a white house straight ahead. Head towards it, but, just before the fence, turn right down steps, go through a KG at the bottom, and, after walking down a few steps, cross the road with care (ST764649).

● *After crossing the road, turn right downhill. After 120m, turn left down steps and carry on down a path. When you come to a road, cross and carry straight on down Sham Castle Lane*, which has a particularly pleasing urban prospect – Bathwick church to the left, the city beyond, and Camden Crescent ahead.

After turning right at the bottom, you will see the Kennet & Avon Canal below you on the left. At the end, bear left and double back along a path towards it. Turn right past the back of a building that once housed the canal company's offices, carry on down to the towpath and go through a tunnel. After emerging in a cutting, turn left through a gate into Sydney Gardens, opened in 1795 and once packed with delights to divert visitors. Standing here during the gardens' heyday, you would have seen, to your left, a maze twice the size of that at Hampton Court, with a Merlin swing in the middle, and a 'romantic subterranean passage' leading to an elaborate grotto. To the right stood a sham castle surrounded by a moat, from which a stream ran to turn the wheel of a miniature mill. All these delights have long gone, although the grotto, dismantled when the railway was built in the late 1830s, seems, after languishing in storage for around 20 years, to have been re-erected by a General Andrews in the garden of his house across the road. Today, his house is the Bath Spa Hotel, and the grotto can still be seen in its grounds.

There is another major difference between the gardens as originally laid out and the gardens today: the trees, many of which would have been mere saplings back then, are now mighty veterans. That means that another of the gardens' attractions – the prospects that could be enjoyed as you walked through them – have been lost as well. If you turn right and walk along to the main path, you will see, up to your right, the truncated remains of a 'lofty pavilion'. A guide to the gardens, published in 1825, described how this commanded

> a view of the Gardens and the surrounding scenery of the metropolis of Somerset; whilst the Kennet and Avon Canal beneath, presents, on its placid bosom, an ever-changing picture, and contributes to the variety and beauty of this enchanting spot. The City, immediately in front, gives an agreeable diversity to the scene, which is bounded by the verdant promontories of the Barrow Hill.[1]

None of which bears much relation to what you see today, while that reference to Barrow Hill seems simply baffling – until, that is, you **head down the path, walk round to the front of the Holburne Museum and look along Great Pulteney Street**, for there, rising above the buildings at the far end, is the unmistakable outline of Twerton Round Hill. Although it is impressive enough from down here, just imagine seeing it from the top of the gardens, over the roof of what was then the Sydney Hotel, with no trees to block the view. In the 18th century, the legend that Twerton Round Hill – or Barrow Hill as it was then known – was the burial mound of Bladud, founder of Bath, was still current. While it is possible that the alignment of Sydney Gardens and Great Pulteney Street with Twerton Round Hill was fortuitous, given that it was regarded as one of the garden's attractions, and given that the whole development was on a greenfield site, there seems no reason to suppose it was not deliberate. More on Twerton Round Hill can be found on pages 191-3, but for now **head along Great Pulteney Street to return to the city centre**.

---

1 Kerr, *Sydney Gardens Vauxhall*

Setting the Scene: Walk 2
Along the Northern Escarpment

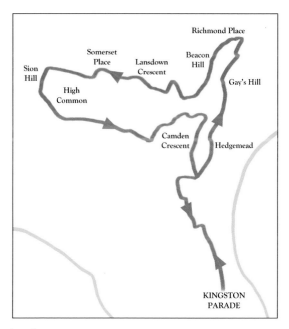

Distance: 4 miles

Terrain: Mostly on pavements and paths, although with some steep steps on which care needs to be taken

Map (optional): OS Explorer 155 or AA Walker's Map 25

Although this walk complements the previous one, it is very different. It could be argued that it does not really belong in a book of country walks, for it is virtually all on hard – albeit sometimes rough – surfaces. Even so, it involves some fairly strenuous climbing, as well as several steep and occasionally broken-down flights of steps.

Until the late 18th century, a walk along Bath's northern escarpment would have been at least as spectacular as a walk along the southern. Since then, development has put paid to many of its rural charms, and, although open spaces do survive, distant views are at something of a

Looking across to Bathampton and Farleigh Downs from Camden Crescent

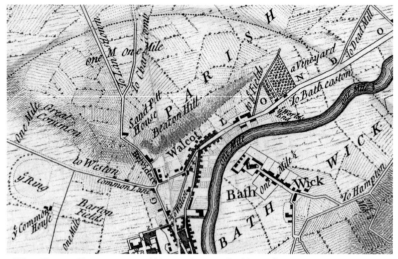

When Thomas Thorpe prepared his map in 1742, Bath's northern escarpment was virtually undeveloped. The only building shown is 'Sand Pitt House' – now the Lansdown Grove Hotel.

premium, not just because they are blocked by houses, but also because of an almost unbroken swathe of vegetation between the houses. Looking back at guidebooks and other accounts from the 19th century, it seems that many views now lost were cherished as much as, if not more than, the city's architectural heritage. And, while the wholesale felling of trees and clearance of vegetation would be not only regrettable but unacceptable, the opening up of selected viewpoints would restore a visual amenity of immense value and historic importance. For now, the only advice is to undertake this walk, if you can, in the winter, when there are less leaves on the trees. That is not to say it is less than delightful at other times of year, but the views, for the most part, are more restricted. However, while there may be frustration aplenty in the early stages, the walk is designed so that the best is saved till last, with an uninterrupted view over a tract of land the developers could not get their hands on – a view that is all the better because you have to wait so long to enjoy it.

From Kingston Parade, head north round the Abbey and carry on along the High Street. Continue along Northgate Street, bearing to the left of St Michael's church to head up Broad Street. At the top, turn left along George Street, and after 50m cross at the pedestrian lights. Carry straight on up Bartlett Street, cross Alfred Street and continue along Savile Row. At the end, cross and turn left along Bennet Street, before turning right up Russel Street. Cross over and turn right at the top, cross Julian Road and turn right past Christ Church. At the end, turn left, bear right over a zebra crossing, and, a little way up the hill, turn right through the gates of Hedgemead Park.

This area, originally known as Edgemead, was covered with rows of terraced cottages in the late 18th and early 19th centuries. The ground, however, was unstable and, between the 1860s and the early 1880s, a series of landslips led to the abandonment of the entire site, after which the council decided that the only thing to do was to turn it into a park.

Follow the path as it curves downhill, and, when it forks, bear left, passing a playground on the right. Carry on past a bandstand, from which you can enjoy a view across to Bathampton Down, *and head up a flight of steps. After crossing a path, go through a gate and bear left uphill. Climb another flight of steps to leave the park, and, after bearing left for a few metres, bear right along a level road,* with Camden Crescent above you. A little way along, you pass Leopold Buildings, which, because of the steepness of the site, appear to have only one storey, but actually have two, as well as the novel feature of upstairs front doors.

Hedgemead Park and Camden Crescent in the early 20th century

At the end, carry straight on up Gay's Hill, passing the former 'Asylum for the Maintenance and Instruction of Young Females in Household Work', founded in 1819 and closed around 1832, but still with a ghost sign on its wall. *At the top, cross and carry on up a steep lane, which, after passing Bellevue Villa on the right and Camden Terrace on the left, dwindles to a footpath.* Just before it curves right, turn to take in a view across the valley to Prior Park.

Follow the path as it curves up to meet a level path, along which you turn right. After going past a gate at the end, bear left up steps and continue up a steep path. A gap in the trees partway up gives a good view across to Bathampton and Farleigh Downs, Bathwick, the Avon valley, Prior Park and Combe Down. *At the top bear left up a final few steps and turn left up a lane.*

After 75m, bear left past bollards and follow a path alongside a hedgerow. To your right, on the far side of Beacon Hill Common, is Richmond Place, at 320m thought to be the longest terrace of Georgian cottages in the country.

A steep climb with only occasional views

When you come to a road, bear left downhill. This is Mount Beacon, several of whose houses date from the late 18th century. Just before the road turns right, you can see where a footpath, known as Jacob's Ladder, and long closed because of subsidence, branched off downhill.

The view from above Jacob's Ladder

Keep straight on instead of bearing right, and, looking through the railings on your left, you should be able to make out its precipitous course. You are on the edge of a cliff even steeper than Beechen Cliff here, although it is difficult to make much out through the trees, even in winter, when the branches are bare. As you carry on, though, the view ahead, towards Twerton, opens up. *When the path broadens into a road and forks, bear right. At the end, bear right again towards St Stephen's church*, which opened – as a chapel of ease – in 1845, It was not consecrated, however – due to its altar being at the north rather than the east end – until 1880.

The crossing at the end is tricky – the easiest way is to cross to St Stephen's, then bear left across to Springfield Place, using the traffic island, before turning left downhill. After 60m, turn right up a couple of steps and head along a path. At the end, go down more steps, through an archway and carry straight on, turning right at the end along Lansdown Crescent.

In 1819, Piers Egan wrote that Lansdown Crescent 'is a noble pile of building; and its extraordinary elevation is the admiration of every spectator, and which completely overlooks the City. By comparison, it is like looking down from the top of St. Paul's Cathedral into the streets of London.' Since then, trees have grown up, drastically restricting the views. Below the crescent, though, sheep still graze as they did two centuries ago. A more recent contribution to this rural prospect comes in the form of several craters, the legacy of bombs dropped here in April 1942.

Lansdown Crescent

At the end of Lansdown Crescent, carry on down Lansdown Place West. Bear right along Somerset Place, where more views open up, *and go down a flight of steps at the end.*

At the bottom, cross the road, turn right downhill, and, at the crossroads, cross and head straight on up Sion Hill. After 250m, turn left by a wall letter-box to continue down Sion Hill. When the road curves right, bear left down a footpath to follow a Cotswold Way signpost across High Common. Here, finally, the views are unrestricted – and superb, not only across to the other side of the valley, but also over to Lansdown Crescent, with Cavendish Crescent below. As you continue down the path, look to the south-west to see the subtle eminence of Twerton Round Hill silhouetted against the horizon.

After 150m, when you come to a path branching left, turn along it. If you look to your right, you can see the back of the Royal Crescent, while up to your left the view of Cavendish and Lansdown Crescents is particularly imposing.

A map of 1810, indicating the direction Great Bedford Street should have taken

At the end, cross the road and head straight on along Park Place. Carry on at the crossroads along Park Street Mews, and, at the end, look to the right down Great Bedford Street, which, as you can see, is aligned on Twerton Round Hill. This street, as you might guess from its name, was to have been much longer, running all the way up to Lansdown Crescent, but, like so many late 18th-century developments, was never completed. *Turn left up St James's Park* – built much later – *and follow it as it curves right. After passing the top of Harley Street, turn left up The Shrubbery* for one final bit of serious climbing (although before you do, it is worth carrying on past it to see Portland Place, one of Bath's least-known Georgian terraces, a few metres further on).

At the top of The Shrubbery, cross the road and head straight on along Lansdown Grove. The Lansdown Grove Hotel, despite all appearances to the contrary, incorporates one of the oldest buildings on Lansdown. The three-storey, five-bay section below the central pediment, now swamped by Victorian and Edwardian additions, was built around 1740 as Sandpit House. *At the end of Lansdown Grove, turn right. After a few metres, you come to a patch of grass where a path, following the original course of Lansdown Road, heads steeply downhill.*

An early 20th-century view of the Lansdown Grove Hotel, whose central section, originally known as Sandpit House, dates from around 1740

The view over Bathwick from above Camden Crescent

Instead of heading down the path, bear left along the road. After a little while, as the trees start to thin out, views open up to your right – first across to Bathampton and Farleigh Downs, before the whole city gradually unfurls below you. *At the end, follow the road as it doubles back downhill round a column. At the bottom, turn right along Camden Crescent*, where palm trees frame the view of Bathampton Down, *and turn left at the end down Lansdown Road*, where one final panorama – of Beechen Cliff – awaits you as you head back into the city.

On the Edge of the City: Walk 3 Along the River & Canal

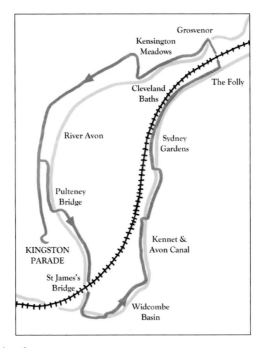

Distance: 4 miles

Terrain: Some steps, but otherwise straightforward

Map (optional): OS Explorer 155 or AA Walker's Map 25

The stretch of river below Pulteney Bridge has long been regarded as one of the jewels in Bath's crown. Upstream, though, a little-known riverside path, tree-lined and secluded, passes through the grounds of once grandiose pleasure gardens, while on the opposite bank the ruins of a more modest rural retreat lie hidden in the undergrowth. These secluded spots, where nature once again holds sway, are the highlight of this short walk, which also includes one of the most scenic stretches of the Kennet & Avon Canal. It starts, though, by visiting the back of Pulteney Bridge, the side few visitors get to see.

Opposite: The Kennet & Avon Canal in Sydney Gardens

From Kingston Parade, head north round the Abbey and carry on along the High Street. Continue along Northgate Street, bearing to the right of St Michael's church to head along Walcot Street. After 125m, just past the Hilton Hotel, turn right through the Cattle Market car park. Turn right at the bottom, before going down steps and continuing along the riverside walkway. Although the buildings rising above you on the right are modern, those that preceded them were no less oppressive. This was the site of the Northgate Brewery, founded around 1776, which grew to become the biggest in the west of England before closing in 1868. Many of the brewery buildings, converted to warehouses and workshops, survived until replaced by the present buildings around 1970.

After climbing a long flight of steps, carry on and turn left across Pulteney Bridge. On the far side of the bridge, cross and turn right down narrow steps leading through an archway to the river. The curious inlet you pass as you bear left along a narrow path is the remnant of a millrace leading to Bathwick Mill. Its ruins survived until the late 1960s when they were swept away, along with the weir that ran diagonally across the river, as part of flood prevention measures.

Spring Gardens – Bath's earliest pleasure gardens – stood where the Beazer Maze and the north end of the Recreation Ground are today. They opened in 1735 and, until Pulteney Bridge was completed in 1774, were reached by ferry. They closed in 1798.

Taken during the big freeze of 1963, this photograph shows the old weir below Pulteney Bridge, togther with the remains of Bathwick Mill

Spring Gardens on a map of 1786

North Parade Bridge as it appeared before being clad in stone in 1936

Carry on under North Parade Bridge, which was built of iron in 1836 and clad in stone in 1936. Across the river, below the end of North Parade, is an arbour, now on the patio of a restaurant, which originally formed part of the riverside gardens attached to Bath's first assembly rooms. Legend has it that Richard Brinsley Sheridan and Elizabeth Linley left notes for each other here before eloping to France in 1772. A little further along, at the end of South Parade, are the remains of steps that once led down to a ferry across the river. Above them, the spire of St John's Roman Catholic church has, since a nesting platform was installed on it in 2005, been home to a breeding pair of peregrine falcons.

Carry on under St James's Bridge, over which the first train linking London with Bath rumbled in 1841, and, *after crossing the canal, turn left past Lower Lock, the first of six that raise the water level almost 20m.* The building beside the lock is an old mill, which predated the canal, but was later converted to pump water partway up the flight of locks. *After going under two road bridges, you have a close-up view of Widcombe Deep Lock*, at 5.92m the second deepest in the country. It was built in 1972 when the two locks that originally stood here – Chapel Lock and Bridge Lock – were removed to accommodate the new road bridge.

Climb the steps beside it, cross the canal via the pavement and continue along the towpath on the other side. Beyond Deep Lock the canal broadens out into Widcombe Basin, once lined with wharves, workshops and warehouses, but now a green space in the heart of the city. *The next lock is known as Wash House Lock; the one beyond it, which you come to after crossing a road by Horseshoes Bridge,*

The canal through Widcombe around 1900. Above: a boat passing through Bridge Lock; below: looking towards Horseshoe Bridge, with Sydney Buildings in the background.

was originally known as Rasamar Lock, but is now called Abbey View Lock. The curiously-wrought column beside it, topped by what appears to be an urn, is actually an old chimney, all that remains of another pumping station that pumped water to the top of the flight. The wide stretch of water beyond is the reservoir – or pound – which supplied it.

After passing the two remaining locks – Second Lock and Top Lock – you will see a couple of old canalside buildings – a coal wharf and a malthouse, both now converted to offices – on the opposite bank. ***When you come to a road bridge, climb a flight of steps, turn right*** *and cross a zebra crossing before continuing along the right bank of the canal.*

After 300m, follow the towpath as it crosses the canal at the back of the former canal company offices and go through a tunnel to emerge in a cutting through Sydney Gardens. Over the tunnel portal is a bust of Sabrina, goddess of the Severn.

After passing under two decorative iron bridges, you come to another tunnel, leading out of Sydney Gardens. The bust above the portal is that of Old Father Thames, which, along with the bust of Sabrina, signified the union of Thames and Severn by the completion of the Kennet & Avon Canal in 1810.

These tunnels were necessary not only because it was originally intended to encircle Sydney Gardens with rows of grand terraces, but also because a gravel ride ran round the gardens. Look out, as you go through the tunnel, for a fascinating collection of mason's marks on its walls. As you emerge into the daylight, an unexpected view opens up before you, with Little Solsbury ahead and the flats of Snow Hill to the left. The canal originally took a different course on leaving the tunnel, curving round to the left in a sweeping arc. Some 30 years later, however, it was rerouted with a tighter curve to make way for the railway. If you look over the wall to your left, you will see the railway below, and, if you look over to the fence beyond the railway, you can see the original course of the canal.

After 600m, you come to a footbridge over the canal. On either side of it, you will see the rotting remains of two stop gates. After passing

Above: The Margherita, which ran pleasure trips between Darlington Wharf and Bradford on Avon in the 1920s, with the old Folly swingbridge in the background

Left: An OS map from the 1880s showing the grounds of the Folly, or Cremorne Gardens as it was then known

Below: Grosvenor Suspension Bridge, opened in 1830 and replaced by the present bridge in 1929

Bath's top lock the canal is level for the next nine miles to Bradford on Avon. As it runs along the side of the Avon valley, for much of this distance there is a bank – often quite a substantial one – on one side of the canal. If part of this bank were to collapse, water would rush through the breach and, if rapid action were not taken, the whole nine-mile stretch would be drained. To prevent this happening, pairs of stop gates, ready to swing shut in either direction should water start flowing through them, were installed all the way along. Today, most appear dilapidated, which raises the question of what would happen if there were to be a breach in the bank.

At one time, there was a swingbridge here, known as Folly Bridge after a pub called the Folly, whose ruins you can see as you *turn down the steps on the left*. The building, which dated from the 18th century, opened as tea gardens, and later as a pub, after the canal was built. In 1862, when a new owner took over the Folly, he opened its extensive grounds as the Cremorne Pleasure Gardens, installing 'the longest and most comfortable bowling alley in Bath' and a 'monster platform' for dancing 'to a full band'. The gardens also featured a large fountain, arbours where refreshments were served and 'Vauxhall lamp' illuminations. The pub even had its own brewery which supplied 'Old English Brewings from the Hampton Springs'. Although the allure of the gardens faded somewhat over time, and the new name was eventually dropped, the Folly survived until May 1942 when a stray German bomber brought its career to an abrupt end. Today, only broken flights of steps, brick walls and piles of stone survive to indicate the site of one of Bath's most enticingly situated hostelries.

At the bottom of the steps, continue under the railway and, after crossing the river via a concrete bridge – which replaced a suspension bridge built in 1830 – turn left, go through a gate and walk down steps to the riverside path. Grosvenor Pleasure Gardens, an enormously ambitious enterprise which opened – although far from ready – in 1792, and closed, after a series of crises, less than ten years later, stood on the right. It extended all the way to Grosvenor Place, the imposing Georgian terrace over to your right, work on which started at the same time. After 200m, you pass the site of a swimming pool which stood at the western end of the gardens, its site now marked by willows and nettles.

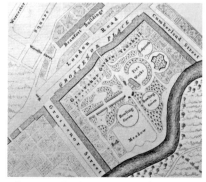

Grosvenor Gardens on a map of 1793

Looking from the riverside path across the site of Grosvenor Pleasure Gardens today
The riverside path beside Kensington Meadows, a green retreat in the heart of the city

A little further on, look out for Cleveland Baths, the country's only surviving Georgian lido, on the opposite bank. Opened in 1817, they closed in 1984, but are now the focus of a reopening campaign. Just beyond them is Bath's Victorian Boating Station, still very much in business. ***When the path forks, bear right to head up to Kensington Meadows.*** The ground level here was originally lower, but was raised when rubble from buildings destroyed by bombing in 1942 was dumped here.

As you ***bear diagonally left to follow a faint track across the meadows***, you will see Kensington Chapel – now converted to housing – in the row of buildings to your left. ***Go through a gap in the fence to the right of metal gates, carry on up to Kensington Place, turn left and continue along the London Road to return to the city centre.***

An Edwardian regatta at Bath Boating Station

In the early 20th century, when the level of Kensington Meadows was lower, water was pumped onto them in cold weather, transforming them into a skating rink when it froze. In this convivial scene, Kensington Chapel can be seen in the background.

On the Edge of the City: Walk 4
The Lost Pleasures of Lyncombe Vale

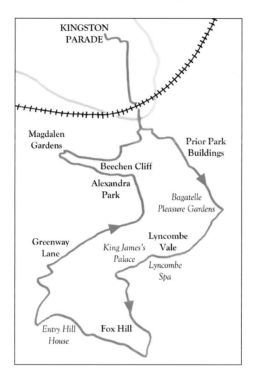

Distance: 3½ miles

Terrain: Muddy, steep and potentially slippery sections, with several flights of steps

Map (optional): OS Explorer 155 or AA Walker's Map 25

This short but by no means undemanding country walk follows the course of the Lyn Brook to discover lost pleasure gardens and an 18th-century spa, before returning to the city through the woods below Beechen Cliff. A word of warning, however – although less than four miles long and on the edge of the city, this walk is challenging in places and good footwear is essential.

Opposite: The path through the woods below Beechen Cliff

From Kingston Parade, head east along York Street. Turn right at the end, bear left along North Parade and right along Pierrepont Street. Continue along Manvers Street and at the end go through a tunnel to the left of the railway station. Carry on across a footbridge over the river and cross the two sets of pedestrian lights ahead. The wide pavement here, and the strip of grass below the wall ahead, was the site of a mill pond fed by the Lyn Brook. It supplied water to Lower Widcombe Mill, which stood beside the river, on the west side of the bridge you have just crossed.

Bear left and after 80m turn right up steps. Turn left at the top along a lane which follows the course of the Lyn Brook. As the lane curves towards the spire of St Matthew's church, you will see another lane running up from the left. It carried on across the brook on a bridge, providing access to what was once a school but has now been converted to flats and renamed Millbrook Court. *Carry on past the gates of Millbrook Court*, following the course of the brook along Millbrook Lane as it curves past the back of a row of early 18th-century cottages built by Ralph Allen for his workers. *At the end, you have to divert slightly to the left before following a path past Prior Park Buildings*, with the brook, no longer culverted, on your left.

At the end of Prior Park Buildings, turn left and then right along Prior Park Road. The brook flows through the grounds of the garden centre on your right before burrowing under the road to Upper Widcombe Mill, which survives as a car showroom. *As the road starts to climb, turn right along Lyncombe Vale*, passing the former Bagatelle pleasure gardens on the right. *Keep to the left-hand pavement along*

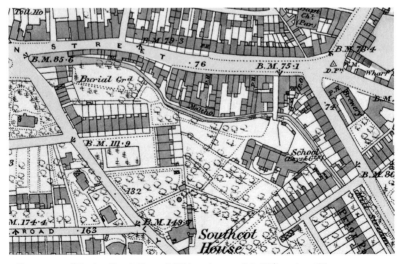

The course of the Lyn Brook through Widcombe on a late 19th-century OS map

Widcombe Crescent from Millbrook Lane

The Lyn Brook flowing past Prior Park Buildings

Lyncombe Vale and you will soon find yourself high above the road, with the brook beside you on the left. Jane Austen walked along this 'raised narrow footpath' in May 1801, describing the scenery, in a letter to her sister, as 'very beautiful'.

After the road rises to meet the pavement, the brook disappears into a culvert by Lyncombe Vale Farm. Just beyond a rustic lodge are the

THE PLEASURE GARDENS OF LYNCOMBE VALE

It was Ralph Allen's decision to commission John Wood to build him a mansion at Prior Park that led to Lyncombe Vale's popularity with 18th-century visitors to Bath. In 1737, four years after work had started on Prior Park, Charles Wicksteed, the proprietor of a toyshop in the Orange Grove, acquired a site adjoining the carriage drive to Prior Park. Here he established a mill, powered by the Lyn Brook, which drove an engraving machine. Known as Wicksteed's Machine, this soon became one of Bath's top attractions, as visitors flocked here to have crests, coats of arms and cyphers engraved on rings, seals, gems and pebbles.

That same year, Charles Milsom, who had rented land further up Lyncombe Vale, discovered a spring which medical experts declared to

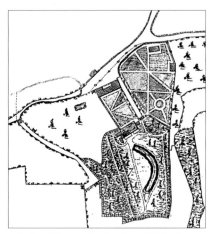

A plan of Lyncombe Spa from 1809, when the estate was sold

be particularly efficacious. Keen to cash in on his discovery, he built a lofty edifice over it, which he opened as Lyncombe Spa (or Spaw) the following year. According to John Wood, however, the foundations of this edifice were so deep that they caused the spring to fail. Curiously, Lyncombe Spa not only survived this setback but seems to have thrived. One possible explanation is that, after the spring failed, Milsom promoted the benefits of a nearby chalybeate spring, as well as the rural delights of the gardens laid out around it, not to mention public breakfasts, French Horn Concerts and the like. Another explanation is that John Wood, peeved at having had his design for a spa building turned down by Milsom, concocted the story, possibly after the spring was diverted, as a result of the building work, to a new course.

Whatever the truth, Lyncombe Spa was still going strong in 1766, when the Rev John Penrose, who had come to Bath from Cornwall to cure his gout, visited. He was so exhausted by the climb, however, that he opted for something stronger than water, and 'was glad of a glass of wine'. The following year, Lyncombe Spa closed to become an inoculation centre for rich visitors anxious to guard themselves against smallpox, but around 1773 became a private house.

By this time, Charles Wicksteed's son had expanded his father's business. In 1769, with the waters of Lyncombe Spa now available only to those seeking inoculation, he decided to exploit a chalybeate spring near the seal-engraving mill, whose waters had 'never failed of curing Consumptive Cases in one Month' and were also good for 'Obstructions, Loss of Appetite, and for bracing relaxed Nerves'.[1]

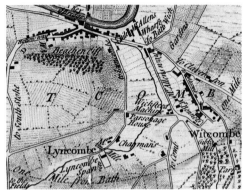

A year later, he opened a pleasure garden called the Bagatelle, which offered musical breakfasts, dancing twice weekly, and delights such as a lamplit waterfall. In 1774, a new owner, James Guillet, took over and installed a 60m men's bathing pool.

Thorpe's map of 1742 showing Wicksteed's Machine – later renamed the Bagatelle – and Lyncombe Spa

It was around this time that the Bagatelle acquired an alternative name – Cupid's Gardens – and a somewhat indecorous reputation. In 1778, it was once again offered for sale. The property consisted of 'two dwelling houses and a summer apartment', plus a garden with 'shrubbery, canal and walks'. 'It is,' an advertisement in the *Bath Chronicle* informed its readers, 'a place of great resort, and much wanted near Bath, but has never yet been conducted with a degree of propriety.'[2]

It was taken by a Mr Harrison from London, who reopened it in June 1778. It closed shortly afterwards, possibly because the lack of propriety which had marked its previous history kept respectable society away.

Visitors to Lyncombe Vale could still find plenty to divert them, however, for in April 1777, a new pleasure garden, known as King James's Palace, opened opposite the former Lyncombe Spa. Its name seems to have derived from a tradition that King James II came to Lyncombe Vale when he visited Bath in 1687. It was kept by Harry Waters, a master tailor who hosted meetings of the Royal Cumberland Masonic Lodge there and also ran what would today be called a garden centre on part of the site. Public breakfasts, concerts and firework displays were held, and 'the best wines, brandy, rum, tea and coffee' were available. The garden, which covered around an acre and a quarter, was also laid out with temples, alcoves, shrubberies and hothouses, but there seems to have been no attempt to market water from the spring which flowed through it. King James's Palace closed, after two changes of ownership, in 1793, a victim of that year's economic crash, bringing the story of Lyncombe Vale's pleasure gardens to a close.

1 *Bath Chronicle*, 20 July 1772
2 *Bath Chronicle*, 19 February 1778

gates of Lyncombe House, opened in 1738 as Lyncombe Spa, but now a school.

Carry on along the road and at the T junction bear left along Lyncombe Vale Road past Lyncombe House. A little further on, as you pass the drive to a house called Westward, look to the right to see a large house on the hillside. Now called Lyncombe Court, it was once surrounded by pleasure gardens known as King James's Palace.

Lyncombe Court, once King James's Palace

From the *Bath Chronicle*, 24 April 1777

KING JAMES'S PALACE,
Opposite LYNCOMB SPAW,
IS neatly fitted up and opened for the reception of Ladies and Gentlemen, by HARRY WATERS.
The best wines, brandy, rum, tea, coffee, &c. Dinners drest at the shortest notice.
To be sold, a great variety of flowers, flower-roots, shrubs, plants, &c.
☞ There will be no illuminations, or fire-works, on the 1st of May as usual; nor will the gates be opened until 5 o'clock in the morning.

A few metres further on, follow a footpath sign up steps on the left. After a crosspath, continue up more steps before following the path as it curves left alongside a fence. When you come to a bridge over the trackbed of the Somerset & Dorset Railway – now the Two Tunnels Greenway – turn right across it (ST752634). *After going through a gate, follow a track bearing slightly to the left up a field where sheep are usually grazing.*

Go through a gate at the top and turn left along a lane. After 150m, when you come to a gatepost for Foxhill Grove, turn right uphill. After another 150m, turn right along a footpath past the back of Foxhill Grove Farm. Carry on, with the fence on your right, along a well-walked track and continue in the same direction through a scrubby field. After 200m, at the end of the field, follow the track as it curves right, with views of Lansdown and Kelston Round Hill ahead.

Continue in the same direction through another field, with views across to Bath's northern crescents, and the lantern of Beckford's Tower just visible above the horizon. After 150m, when the path forks, bear right and carry on through the remains of an old kissing gate (KG) (ST749631). *Continue down a broad path with widely-spaced steps beside a wall,* behind which, partway down, can be glimpsed the baronial Gothic splendour of Entry Hill House. After passing some magnificent beeches, ***carry on down into Lyncombe Vale. Continue along a lane for a few metres, before turning right to follow a footpath sign by a house called Lynden.*** After 150m, you will see, through a fence ahead, the Lyn Brook issuing from a culvert. ***Carry on between fences and after 75m, when you come to another path, turn left up it.***

As the path climbs out of the valley, it gives way to ever steeper steps. At the top, turn right along Greenway Lane. After 100m, go through a KG on the left and bear right through playing fields. The

circular building behind the wall a little way along on the left, built as a Georgian summerhouse in a garden on Devonshire Place, is believed to have been used as a synagogue in the late 19th century.[1] ***At the end of the field, go through a gap in the hedge and continue through a KG. Carry on through a field and follow a track as it curves left alongside a fence to emerge in another field with extensive views.***

Go through a KG at the end and turn left up a path into Alexandra Park where a viewing platform overlooks the city. ***Carry on along a path at the edge of the escarpment, which, after 150m, leaves the park to continue past the***

The Georgian summerhouse
on Devonshire Place

backs of houses. At the end, turn right down steps. Carry on down a path and, after more steps, turn right into Magdalen Gardens, where volunteers have effected an extraordinary transformation of this long neglected spot. Opposite is St Mary Magdalen Chapel, which had its origins in a leper hospital founded in the 12th century.

At the end of the park, go up a short flight of steps and continue along a path. After crossing another path, carry on through the woods, past the graffiti-covered walls of ruined cottages and a disintegrating World War Two air-raid shelter.

Eventually the path leads down steps. At the bottom, head across to a large house on the far side of a patch of grass and turn right down the road. Turn left down Lyncombe Hill and right at the bottom, before crossing at the pedestrian lights and retracing your steps to the city centre.

1 The history of the building can be found at bearflathistory.com/wp-content/uploads/2013/05/The-Temple.pdf.

North to the High Hills: Walk 5 Kelston Round Hill, Saltford & the Avon Navigation

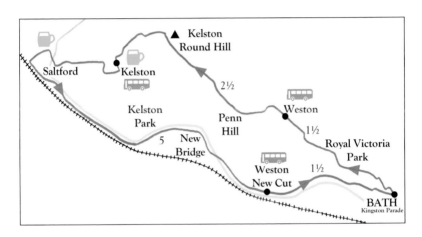

Distance: 10½ miles;
  shorter options available by:
  catching a bus (4 or 9) from Bath to Weston at the start;
  catching a bus (19 or 37) from Kelston back to Bath;
  or catching a bus (X39, etc) from Locksbrook to Bath at the end

Terrain: Mostly straightforward and on well-walked footpaths, but with seven stiles; livestock may be encountered on Kelston Round Hill

Pubs and cafés:
  Old Crown, Kelston; food served all day Tue-Sun (baguettes only from 3 to 6pm weekdays) (oldcrownkelston.com; 01225 423032)

  Bird in Hand, Saltford; open all day; food served 11-2.30 Mon-Fri, 11-9 Sat & Sun (www.birdinhandsaltford.co.uk; 01225873335)

Map: OS Explorer 155 or AA Walker's Map 25

Opposite: The track leading down from Kelston Round Hill

43

This walk heads out through Weston to Kelston Round Hill, the most prominent and distinctive high point in north-east Somerset, which commands superb views in all directions. From there it heads down to Kelston village, whose fascinating collection of ancient buildings includes a popular country pub and the outbuildings of a long-demolished Elizabethan mansion. From Kelston, there is the option of returning to Bath by bus, or of carrying on across the Avon to Saltford.

Two centuries ago, Pierce Egan dismissed Saltford contemptuously, declaring that it 'contains but a few straggling houses'; anyone whose experience of Saltford is confined to driving through it along the main road may be inclined to agree with him. Exploring the village on foot, however, reveals hidden treasures, including the oldest continuously occupied private house in the country, a tiny church with a bizarre and haunting memorial, a former beerhouse where Brunel's navvies slept, and an 18th-century brass mill.

Then it is back to Bath, following a riverside path along which gangs of men once towed heavily-laden boats. En route, we pass Kelston Park, high on a bluff above the river. This grand house, which replaced Kelston's Elizabethan mansion, was designed by John Wood the Younger and is set in grounds landscaped by Capability Brown. There is also plenty of opportunity to admire the engineering genius of Isambard Kingdom Brunel, whose Great Western Railway (GWR) runs alongside the towpath.

Bath's other railway – the Midland – is not forgotten, either, as two bridges on this long-closed line are used to cross and recross the river. Finally, on the outskirts of the city, we pass one of Bath's least-known, but most impressive, Georgian bridges before following a path alongside one of the earliest stretches of canal in the country.

From Kingston Parade, head to the left of the Abbey, cross Abbey Church Yard, and, after passing under the colonnade, turn right along Stall Street. Carry on along Union Street and, at the top, turn left along Upper Borough Walls. At the end, turn right up Barton Street and continue up the east side of Queen Square, before crossing at the lights to head up the left-hand side of Gay Street. Take the first left along Queen's Parade Place, and, at the end, turn right through gates guarded by lions to walk along Royal Avenue. Go through gates guarded by sphinxes at the far end, cross the road, and carry on past the obelisk.

Continue past a road bearing right, but, a little further on, take a path on the right heading across the park. Carry on across a tarmac path, cross a road, turn left along a footpath and bear right when it forks. Behind the railings on your left is the Great Dell, a woodland glade established in an old quarry, where the gigantic head of Jupiter, carved in 1831, can be seen through the trees.

Turn left when you reach the main road, cross the zebra crossing and carry on in the same direction along Weston Road. After 350m, follow the main road as it bears right, before turning left along Weston Park. Carry on in the same direction when you come to Weston High Street. At the end, cross the zebra crossing and carry straight on up Penn Hill Road to the left of the old Crown & Anchor.

If travelling from the city centre by bus, get off in Weston High Street and walk up Penn Hill Road to the left of the old Crown & Anchor.

At the top of Penn Hill Road, bear right along the main road and carry on across the end of Southlands. A few metres further on, go up steps and through a kissing gate (KG) to follow a Cotswold Way (CW) signpost across a playing field.

Head to the right of the left-hand goalposts, making for a gap in the hedge, where you will find a KG (ST724663). *Go through it, head straight up a field, go through a handgate and continue up a farm track between fences, passing a trig point (121m above sea level) on the left with a good view southward. Carry on through another handgate and follow a path winding along the top of a field, with a view across to Beckford's Tower.*

Cross a stile and head up a lane (ignoring a turning to the left), and, as you carry on along the CW, Kelston Round Hill, topped by a

Kelston Round Hill

KELSTON ROUND HILL

It is hard to believe, standing atop Kelston Round Hill on a clear day, that this Silbury-like eminence was not regarded with awe and reverence in prehistoric times. Yet, if it did generate any legends, none has come down to us, nor does it feature alongside the other high places around Bath in John Wood's mythico-psychogeographical cosmology of the city.

The earliest account of the hill seems to be that of the Rev John Collinson, who in 1791 described it as

> a fine eminence called Henstridge-hill, and sometimes Kelston Round-hill, which rises to a vast height above the bed of the river. The upper part of it has the appearance of a very large tumulus, and on its top is a plantation of firs, inclosed by a circular wall. This spot commands a prospect very extensive, and as finely varied with grand and pleasing scenery as most in the county.

The only thing to have changed is the enclosure on the summit, which is now surrounded by a fence rather than a wall, and contains a variety of deciduous trees, including beech and ash, instead of firs. Collinson's comparison of the upper part of it to 'a very large tumulus' is interesting – was he hedging his bets, perhaps, implying that it could be man-made, without actually saying so? There may well have been tumuli or other prehistoric structures on top of the hill, but the planting of trees would have destroyed them – and, if this was the case, it begs the question as to whether the trees were planted to improve the view or to eradicate unwelcome traces of paganism.

Another – and far more appealing – possibility is that the walled plantation was designed not to destroy but to enhance what was already there. Could the hill, perhaps, have been crowned, in ancient times, by a sacred grove, to which only the elect were admitted? And was the 18th-century planting a recreation of such a grove, or a modification of one that already stood there, whose origins dated back not centuries but millennia?

Despite the absence of historical records – or legends – Kelston Round Hill's distinctive profile, dominating the horizon from both Bath and Bristol, and the magnificent views from its summit, have earned it a special place in the hearts and minds of many who live within sight of it. And, although its magic and mystery long remained uncelebrated, an old barn below the hill has recently been converted to a meeting place, dedicated to 'celebration, reflection, creative and artistic purposes'. In July 2016, Three Cane Whale, a Bristol-based band, got together with poet Jon Hamp 'to reflect upon and connect with the spirit of the hill' at a gig in the barn. It was recorded and is now available from kelstonrecords.co.uk, while more information on the old barn and some superb photographs of the hill can be found at kelstonroundhill.com.

The view over Weston from Kelston Round Hill

clump of trees, comes into view ahead. After 1150m, bear left through a KG and follow a permissive path to the top of Kelston Round Hill, where a bench is provided to take in the view over Bath, with the Westbury White Horse on the distant horizon. At certain times of year, you may notice a spring issuing from the ground here, making the area in front of the bench surprisingly muddy.

Bear left alongside the fence surrounding the trees, passing a trig point (218m above sea level), and cross a stile. When you come to another bench, with a view westward, make your way down a faint track, heading for a small white noticeboard in the hedgerow in the corner of the field (ST709677).

Cross a stile and bear left down a high-banked track, which turns into a tarmac lane as you pass Coombe Barn Cottages. Continue down the lane and, at the main road, turn left through Kelston village. The

initials you can see on the cottages are those of Colonel Inigo Jones, the local landowner, who had them built in the mid-19th century. Look out for an impressive ammonite on the wall of the old forge and a truncated elephant's head on the water trough. A little further on is the Old Crown, one of the most popular traditional pubs around Bath. 👉

If you want to end the walk here, you can catch a bus back to Bath from outside the Old Crown.

Otherwise, carry on along the road past the old lock-up, where those who imbibed too freely were incarcerated until they sobered up,

'Mr Harrington's' manor appears on Thorpe's 1742 map, along with Hen Stretch – a corruption of Henstridge – Hill, the old name for Kelston Round Hill

and turn right alongside the wall of Tower House. This Italianate villa, dating from the 1830s, was built as a dower house for Kelston Park, which you will be seeing later.

After passing 17th-century Park Farm, the home of Bath Soft Cheese, look to the left to see a 16th-century outbuilding once attached to Kelston Manor. *After passing the Old Rectory, turn left past the village hall* – another former outbuilding – and, as you enter the churchyard, look to the right to see a converted barn dating from the time when Kelston was owned by Shaftesbury Abbey.

To the east of the church – 13th century but ruthlessly restored in the mid-19th, albeit with some splendidly fiendish gargoyles – is the Inigo Jones family vault. In the field beyond it stood Kelston Manor, demolished in the late 18th century. The two raised areas you can see on the far side of the field are the site of the formal gardens that stood behind it.

After heading to the west side of the churchyard to see more converted outbuildings, including a 17th-century dovecote reputed to have had the largest number of nesting boxes in Somerset, *retrace your steps along the lane leading away from the church and turn left at the end.*

The thatched building you pass on the left, now known as Tatters, dates from the 17th century, if not earlier, and was once the Cock Inn – possibly because cockfights were held there – before becoming a post office in the 19th century. In its north gable end is an old timber-framed

THE METAMORPHOSES OF KELSTON

In the middle ages, Kelston – or Kelweston, as it was known – formed part of the estate of Shaftesbury Abbey. After the dissolution, Henry VIII granted Kelston to Ethelreda Malte, the illegitimate daughter of his tailor, John Malte. At least that was the official line. It is more likely that she was Henry's illegitimate daughter, hence his generosity to her, which also extended to the gift of St Catherine's Court, north of Batheaston, which was previously owned by Bath Abbey. In 1546 or 1547, Ethelreda married a courtier called John Harington, and bore him a daughter, before dying in her late twenties. John Harington remarried, and around 1570 started work on a new house at Kelston. Designed by the celebrated architect Giacomo Barozzi da Vignola, it was described as 'the largest house at that time in Somersetshire'. John Harington did not live to see it completed, however. That was left to his son by his second marriage, Sir John Harington, poet, wit, courtier, godson to Queen Elizabeth, and, by virtue of a pamphlet called *A New Discourse of a Stale Subject, called the Metamorphosis of Ajax*, popularly regarded as the inventor of the flush toilet. The inclusion of Ajax in the title was a pun on 'jakes', a slang word for a privy. When Queen Elizabeth visited Bath in 1592, she stayed at Kelston, not just because Harington was her godson, but because it was, in John Wood's words, 'the Flower of all the Manors within the City of Bath in its antient State'.

Sir John Harington died in 1612, but the house remained in the family until 1759, when it was sold to Sir Caesar Hawkins, sergeant-surgeon to King George III. Harington's house, grand though it was, was by now somewhat antiquated. Even worse, for a fashion-conscious Georgian, it did not have much of a view. There was, however, a summerhouse, half a mile south of the house, on an eminence high above the river. It was here that Hawkins commissioned John Wood the Younger to build him a new

mansion, called Kelston Park. Once it was complete, the old house was torn down, leaving only the ghostly outline of the gardens which stood behind it, together with a few outbuildings.

In 1828, Kelston Park was bought by Joseph Neeld, an MP and property developer, who also bought Grittleton Manor near

One of the surviving outbuildings of Kelston Manor

Chippenham in the same year. Although he rebuilt Grittleton in Gothic Revival style, he made few changes at Kelston, which, on his death in 1856, was inherited by his son-in-law, Colonel Inigo Jones, whose initials can be seen on many of the estate buildings around Kelston. In 1967, Kelston Park was leased to the Methodist Church for use as a training centre, but in 1993, by now in poor condition, it was purchased by Andrew Brownsword, and since restoration has been used as offices.

window, originally unglazed and recalling the original meaning of 'window' as a 'wind eye' or 'wind hole'. On your right, the old school, with a datestone of 1863, is now a luxury hotel for cats.

Go through a handgate, passing stables with an ammonite in the gable end, and continue through another handgate straight ahead. Carry on between a fence and a hedge, and, at the end, where there is a choice of gates, go through a KG on the left to walk alongside a hedge. Continue through another KG and at the end carry on along a concrete farm track. After 250m, continue through two more KGs (although the gates beside them may be open), and, after another 250m, go through a KG and carry on towards a bridge in the railway embankment ahead (ST688672).

Just before the bridge, go through a KG on the right to climb the embankment, turn left across the bridge and right onto a path on the old trackbed of the Midland Railway line from Bath to Bristol. Kelston station, opened at the insistence of Colonel Inigo Jones, over whose land the line was built, stood just along to the left. It was accessible only on foot and closed in 1949. *Turn right along the railway path, and, after crossing the river, bear left down steps to the car park of the Bird in Hand pub* 🍺 *and turn left uphill into Saltford village.*

The Bird in Hand was originally a pair of thatched cottages, and converted to a pub when the railway opened in 1869. There was a footpath alongside the line and over the bridge to Kelston station, which meant it was much handier for the villagers of Saltford than it was for Colonel Inigo Jones's tenants in Kelston. As you carry on past the pub up the High Street, you are walking through the oldest part of the village, with some exceedingly venerable cottages tucked away between more recent buildings.

To your left, on the corner of The Batch, the Brass Knocker, with a datestone of 1747, was another pub which opened around the same time as the Bird in Hand, albeit only with a licence to sell beer. It was also a grocer's, a butcher's, and, in the early 20th century, a post office.

On the right, by the old school, is Queen Square – less impressive than the Queen Square you passed through earlier, but leading to something of exquisite rarity. Saltford Manor, thought to be the oldest

Saltford Manor

continuously occupied private house in England, dates from around 1160. Although none of the original building can be seen from the front, if you **head through the churchyard** and look back when you reach the end, you will see a Norman window framed by two buttresses, as well as other medieval work.

The church is another hidden gem. Its demure tranquillity gives no hint of its troubled history, yet it was so knocked around in the Civil War that much of it had to be rebuilt, after almost two centuries of semi-dereliction, in the 19th century. Parliamentary soldiers also carried away and defaced the font, which was discovered years later in use as a cattle trough on Lansdown.

Perhaps the most remarkable thing in the church, though, is a tombstone in the porch which reads:

> Stop Reader: a wonder see
> As strange as ere was known
> My feet dropt off from my body
> In the midst of the bone
> I had no Surgeon for my help
> But God Almighty's Aid
> On whom I allways will rely
> And never be afraid
> Tho here beneath Interd they ly
> Corruption for to see
> Yet they shall Rise and Reunite
> To all Eternity
> Frances Flood April 1st 1723

Kelston Round Hill from Saltford churchyard

Frances Flood came from near Honiton in Devon. In the spring of 1723, she arrived in Saltford from Norton St Philip and stayed the night at an inn. She set off next morning, but did not get very far before falling ill, and, after applying to the overseer of the poor for aid, which was refused, she took refuge in a 'hog sty'. She later recorded the numerous indignities and extremities she suffered over the ensuing weeks in horrific detail; she had contracted smallpox, and, although she survived, the appalling conditions she had to endure led to the loss of both of her legs after gangrene set in. On her recovery, she wrote a tract entitled *The Devonshire Woman; or a Wonderful Narrative of Frances Flood*, which was 'Printed for Frances Flood and sold by Nobody but herself'. Although now an exceedingly rare document, this remarkable account of an extraordinary woman's triumph over appalling adversity can be found on the internet.

Head back through Queen Square and turn right uphill. At 18 High Street, on the corner of Homefield Close, was the Railroad Arms Beerhouse, opened when the GWR was being built through the village. As well as serving beer, its attic was converted to a dormitory sleeping around 20 navvies.

Before turning up the drungway beside it, carry on up the High Street for a little way to see two grand Georgian Houses – Saltford House, with a datestone of 1771, and Tunnel House, bought by Isambard Kingdom Brunel in 1836 so that he could build a tunnel beneath it.

Returning to the drungway, head up it and carry on as it runs beside a high fence with the GWR in a cutting below. After 150m, when you come to a footpath on the left, turn along it, to see Kelston Round Hill straight ahead. **Go through a KG at the end, turn right and head along a footpath to the right of a house called The Ridge. After 40m, just before a house called Rosemere, turn left.** From here, there is a view not only of Kelston Round Hill, but also of the Midland Railway bridge you crossed earlier. At the end, when the path swings right, there is also a good view of Kelston weir.

After walking down steps, carry on in the same direction for a few metres, before turning left down a steep flight of steps to the river, where a ferry operated until the 1920s. The ferryman lived in the one of the cottages on the left.

It has been claimed that Saltford got its name because, before mills were built downstream, the Avon was tidal to this point and salt water flowed up to it. However, it is now thought that it was where a 'salt way', along which salt from Droitwich was carried to the south-west, forded the river. Salt was once a valuable commodity, and salt ways, often

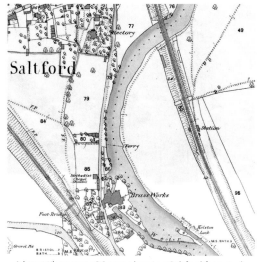

A late 19th-century OS map showing Saltford ferry and brass mill, Kelston Lock and Kelston station

dating back to pre-historic times, existed in many parts of the country. The route of a salt way can still be traced between Cranham and Sheepscombe in Gloucestershire, while the village of Salford Priors in Warwickshire – once known as Saltford – got its name because it stood where the salt way from Droitwich to Hillborough crossed the River Arrow.

Recent research has also indicated that a salt way ran from Saltford to Camerton.[1]

Turn right past a restored 18th-century brass mill, one of several that once operated along the river between Bath and Bristol. It ceased production in the 1920s, but still has its furnace and waterwheel. Major restoration projects were carried out by volunteers in 1995 and 2014, and the mill can be visited on regular open days.[2]

Just past the brass mill, follow a footpath leading down steps on the left to a riverside path (ST687669). This leads past the weir, on the far side of which is Kelston Lock, one of six built between Bath and Hanham in 1727 to make the river navigable. *After passing the Riverside pub, a footbridge with steep steps leads over the entrance to a marina. Carry on past boathouses and follow the path between river and railway,* enjoying a pastoral idyll broken only by the sound of occasional trains rushing past.

After 1750m, the path crosses the Corston Brook. Just before it, where the towpath switched from the north to the south bank, was the site of a ferry which carried horses across the river. When the river was made navigable in 1727, the towpaths were not suitable for use by horses, and gangs of men had to tow the boats. When the towpath switched banks, as it did several times, the men simply hopped onto the

1 See Priston Village Design Statement 2016 ; also a talk by Clare Cross to the Priston History Group on 31 January 2013 (www.priston.org.uk)

2 At time of writing these take place on the 2nd and 4th Saturdays of the month from May to October between 10am and 4pm (see www.brassmillcom for more information).

boats to get across. Horses were less accommodating, so when the towpath was upgraded around 1812, a series of horse ferries had to be introduced as well.

The river now curves away from the GWR line to go under the old Midland Railway line, with Kelston Park high above. The site

The Avon below Kelston Park

Sir Caesar Hawkins chose for the mansion he built to replace Kelston's Elizabethan manor house could hardly have been more spectacular. Lancelot Brown, celebrated for seeing 'capabilities' for improvement in the most uninspiring landscapes, was faced, on arrival at Kelston, with one that hardly needing improving. Even so, by judicious planting of trees, he created something that, over two centuries later, still conveys an air of Georgian serenity and grandeur. In 1791, the Rev John Collinson wrote that, 'from the point of the hill on which the house stands, a fine lawn, interspersed with single trees, extends to the river, which here forms a fine curve through one of the richest vales in the world, and is then lost to the eye under the hanging woods, which vest the declivity of the hill to the south and west.' Despite two railways having been built through this sequestered vale, it is a description that still holds true over 200 years later.

New Bridge

A little further along, after passing another grand 18th-century house – Beaulieu Lodge – on the edge of the escarpment, the New Bridge comes into view ahead. It is a suitably impressive entrance to a World Heritage city, yet, because it is so far from the centre, is surprisingly little known. Work on it started in 1735, but, following modifications and repairs, it was widened and reprofiled a century later. *Follow the footpath through a small arch in the embankment of the bridge and carry on. When the path forks, bear right up steps and left along the former Midland Railway line to cross the river. Once across, bear right to head down to the riverside path.*

After 750m, you come to Weston Cut, a 500m canal built in 1727 to avoid two weirs. It was provided not only with a lock but also with a waterside inn, originally known as the Dolphin, but now renamed the Locksbrook Inn. The island created when Weston Cut was built was known as Dutch Island, because of the number of skilled workers from the Low Countries who came over to work in the brass mills established on it. A bus depot now covers most of the island.

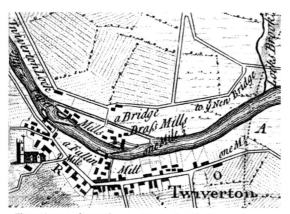

Thorpe's map of 1742 showing Weston Cut, the brass mills on Dutch Island and the village of Twerton – then known as Twiverton

To catch a bus to the city centre, bear left before the Locksbrook Inn up Avondale Road, cross the Upper Bristol Road and turn left to the bus stop.

Otherwise, carry on, as Weston Cut rejoins the river, and after 1300m, just after passing under a suspension bridge, bear left to follow a road leading away from the river. Head to the left of Norfolk Crescent (which you will see ahead) to carry on along Great Stanhope Street and New King Street. At the end, cross at the pedestrian lights, bear left, carry straight on across the lights at the top and turn right. Take the first left by the Griffin pub, bear right through Beaufort Square, carry on along Trim Street, follow it as it bears right at the end and turn left along Upper Borough Walls. At the end, turn right along the High Street to return to the starting point.

North to the High Hills: Walk 6
Lansdown & the Woolley Valley

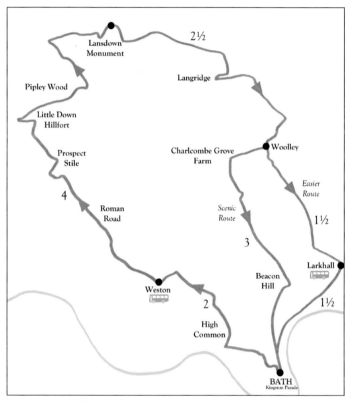

Distance: 11½ miles;
  shorter options available by:
  catching a bus (4 or 9) from Bath to Weston at the start of the walk;
  catching a bus (7 or 6a) from Larkhall to Bath at the end of the walk

Terrain: Some steep sections and stiles; sheep and cattle likely at certain
  points

Pubs and cafés: None

Map: OS Explorer 155 or AA Walker's Map 25

Opposite: The green lane from Lansdown to Langridge

This walk takes in some of the finest scenery around Bath, ranging from far-reaching views to hidden valleys, and from the windy bleakness of the Cotswold edge to the lush pastures of the Woolley valley. It also contains plenty of historical interest: the site of the Battle of Lansdown, a Roman road, an iron age hillfort, a Norman church, gunpowder mills and a church designed by John Wood the Younger.

It also includes two stiff climbs, although there is the option of avoiding the second one by taking a more leisurely route along a country lane before catching a bus back to the city centre. There is also the option of catching a bus to Weston from Bath and starting the walk there.

Unfortunately, there are no pubs, cafés, shops or other facilities en route, and, as climbing up to and walking across Lansdown, especially on a hot day, can be a tiring business, it is strongly recommended that, at the very least, you carry some water with you.

From Kingston Parade, head to the left of the Abbey, cross Abbey Church Yard, go through the colonnade and turn right along Stall Street. Carry on up Union Street and at the top turn left along Upper Borough Walls. At the end, turn right up Barton Street and continue up the east side of Queen Square, before crossing at the lights to head up the left-hand side of Gay Street. Take the first left along Queen's Parade Place, and, at the end, turn right through gates guarded by lions and walk along Royal Avenue. Go through gates guarded by sphinxes at the end, cross the road, and head past the obelisk. Just beyond it, turn right up a road. Go through the gateposts at the top, continue over a zebra crossing and go through a gateway to follow a path beside an iron fence straight ahead across High Common.

At the top, turn left along Sion Hill to follow the Cotswold Way (CW). Turn left at the top along Summerhill Road, and, at the end, carry straight on along a drungway with a CW sign. Just before heading down steps, you pass the entrance to the Retreat, which, for those lucky enough to have known it, is one of Bath's most fondly-remembered pubs. It closed in 1975 but its vine-cloaked sign bracket still stands above the entrance.

Cross Primrose Hill and carry straight on down a path. After crossing a brook at the bottom, go through a kissing gate (KG) and carry on, following CW waymarks. Go through a handgate by a seven-bar metal gate, and, when the path forks, bear left. At the end of the field, go through a KG and turn left (ST733665). *Carry on down an access road, and, after crossing another road, continue down a footpath. When you come to Weston churchyard, go through a gap in the wall and follow a path to the left of the church. After passing the church, carry on down a footpath with a metal handrail and continue along the pavement. At the end, head to the left of a building with a ghost sign advertising cigarettes, cross the zebra crossing and continue along the High Street.*

If catching a bus from the city centre, get off in Weston High Street and continue along the High Street.

After 300m, you pass the old Globe at Nº 82 – the smallest pub in Bath, until it closed in 1966. *At the roundabout, bear left and carry straight on along Deanhill Lane for 200m, before turning right along Osborne's Lane. After 250m, at the entrance to Lansdown Grange Farm, turn right to follow a footpath across a bridge over the West Brook. Follow the path as it bears left alongside the brook before crossing back over it a little further on. After climbing steps, the path narrows and goes through a gate to pass the end of a row of cottages.* Until recently, the path went through the cottage at the end; you can still see where the entrances were filled in to create an extra room.

Go through another gate and carry on with a hedge on your right. At the end of the field, cross a stile and carry on along a lane. When the lane forks by Redstile Cottage, carry straight on. The lane turns increasingly rough, and, after going through a handgate by a four-bar gate, starts winding steeply uphill. Although it may not look it, this is believed to have been the Roman road from Bath to Portus Abonae (Sea Mills), from where soldiers embarked for the legionary fortress at Caerleon. As you climb, you will see Kelston Lock and weir far below.

A view of the Avon valley from above Prospect Stile

After a particularly steep section, the lane swings right before bearing left through a gate, where it narrows dramatically. After passing a handgate on the left, carry on through another handgate, before turning through a high gate on the right into Shiner's Wood nature reserve (ST712680). *Carry on up to another KG and bear left up to Prospect Stile* , from which, according to John Wood, writing in 1742, you could 'behold ... a region that sets paradise itself before one's eyes'. Today, a topograph has been installed to indicate the location of various landmarks, including the White Horse at Westbury.

Go through a KG – a replacement for the original stile – *and bear left alongside a wall, with Bath racecourse* – the highest flat racecourse in the country – *on your right. After 250m, carry straight on through a gap in a fence*, keeping a lookout for another glimpse of Kelston Lock far below, *and at the end bear right to follow the ramparts of Little Down hillfort. After 150m, bear left through the ramparts to head across the iron age fort. After going through a KG on the far side* (ST707689)*, the view westward over Bristol opens up.*

Continue downhill a little way before bearing right alongside the fence. Carry on through a KG, before joining a broader track which at some time has been paved. Given the number of Roman remains that have been found in this area, it may well date back to Roman times, although the paving visible today is almost certainly more recent.

The valley to your left is Pipley Bottom, where stepped terraces, created by the Romans to cultivate vines, can still be seen on south-facing slopes. Rocky outcrops up to your right, meanwhile, appear to be

The view westward over Pipley Bottom

the legacy of small-scale quarrying. *After going through another gate, carry on with the manicured greens of the golf course on your right and the gloriously unmanicured fastnesses of Pipley Wood on your left.* This 60-acre ancient woodland, clinging to steep slopes running with muddy springs, richly rewards exploration, but, as the only two entrances are at the top, any walk through it has to be circular (visit pipleywood.com for more information).

Carry on in the same direction, following signs for the CW. At the end of Pipley Wood, head straight on across the golf course, passing a stone barn on your right. When you come to a broad crosspath, bear left, following a CW waymark.

Carry on for 600m, and, after the path curves down to the left, follow the CW up through a small wooden gate on the right

Looking north from Hanging Hill

(ST715698). *Carry on through a KG, with the hedge on your left, to the edge of Hanging Hill and the first of a series of interpretation panels for Lansdown Battlefield.* In 1819, Pierce Egan wrote that 'this part of Somersetshire has often been compared to some of the picturesque and enchanting prospects in Switzerland' and was 'as fertile in scenery as the most lively imagination can suggest'. Yet, however magnificent the views, appreciation of them will always be tempered by the memory of 5 July 1643, when Royalist troops fought an uphill battle against Parliamentary forces entrenched in a commanding position on the edge of the escarpment. It is not easy to imagine what it must have been like, struggling up these precipitous slopes in high summer, burdened with weapons, being fired on from above, with your comrades falling around you.

Despite heavy losses, the Royalists finally gained a foothold on top of the hill, forcing the Parliamentarians to withdraw. Yet, although they won the day, it was a Pyrrhic victory: it is estimated that between 200 and 300 Royalist soldiers were killed and many more injured, while the Parliamentarians lost only around 20 men, with around 60 wounded.[1]

1 See Wroughton, *The Battle of Lansdown: An Explorer's Guide*

Go through a KG and turn right. The path leads into woodland and through a gate. When you reach a drive, turn right along it, go through a KG on the left and continue along a path. Another gate leads back onto the drive, along which you turn left. At the main road, cross with care to a lay-by and follow a path to a monument commemorating Sir Bevil Grenville, who fell, mortally wounded, at the head of a Cornish infantry regiment, as they gained the summit of the hill. In 1720, on the spot where he fell, his grandson, Henry Grenville, Lord Lansdown, erected this monument in his memory (ST722703).

The griffin on the Grenville Monument

The woods north of the monument

Carry on past the monument, following a path curving through woodland. Cross a stepped stile, carry on beside a wall, cross another stepped stile at the end and carry on downhill. Once through a seven-bar gate, the path turns into a green lane. After 350m, when the CW bears left (ST730703)*, carry straight on along the lane*, which, considering the number of packhorses, people and wagons that have passed along it – not to mention the amount of water which has coursed down it – is in remarkably good shape. Although it would come as something of a shock if you were to encounter a dust-spattered cavalier trotting past on his steed, he would hardly seem out of place, so little has this forgotten byway changed over the centuries. Lanes such as this can, if you are alive to their resonances, be wormholes into the past. But they do not just evoke nostalgia for a distant past; in their persistence and continuity, they can seem prefigurations of a time where human endeavour will focus not on the destruction of the natural world but once more of working in harmony with it.

The path leading down from the monument

When you come to a T junction, turn right past an old barn and follow a lane downhill. At the bottom, by Tyning Cottage, there is a short – and well worthwhile – diversion to the Norman church and medieval court at Langridge.

● *If you decide to give the diversion a miss, turn left here and skip the next paragraph.*

● *To visit Langridge, turn right and after 200m you will see the church on your right, with the court just beyond. From here, retrace your steps along the lane and carry on past Tyning Cottage.*

The church of St Mary Magdalene, Langridge

LANGRIDGE

In 1940, Arthur Mee wrote that 'there is no more delightful experience for an Englishman than to be lost in some of the lanes around Bath, and if it is in the valley by the Gloucester Road it is all the better ... When we come to Langridge there is nothing about us but the lovely group made by the barn, the farmhouse, and the church. Dull would he be of soul who could pass by a sight so touching in its tenderness.'

Mee is not the only writer to have waxed lyrical about this spot. In his 1848 book of *Rambles about Bath*, James Tunstall wrote that the road down to Langridge 'traverses one of the most beautiful passes in the neighbourhood of the city. Were it not for the fertility of the hill sides, we might imagine ourselves in one of those beautiful glens which diversify the scenery of Cumberland or Lancashire.' Even the generally restrained Rev John Collinson described Langridge as 'situated ... on the eastern declivity of Lansdown, with a rich and beautiful vale below.'

It is extraordinary how a place so close to Bath can still seem so remote. Walking the grass-grown lanes of this hidden valley is to take

a trip back in time. Few of the houses you pass are later than the 17th century, and some are considerably older. Much of the fabric of the church is Norman, although the apse at its east

Langridge Court Farm

end was added by Major Davis (who also built Bath's Empire Hotel) in 1872. Along with memorials to members of the Blathwayt family, its treasures include a 13th-century carving of the Madonna and Child. Sadly, one of its greatest treasures, a medieval brass depicting Elizabeth Walsche, with a small dog at her feet, was stolen in 2002.

Court Farm, next to the church, dates from the 14th century, although, given how long this valley has been settled, it may well stand on the site of a much older building. Roman coins of the 4th century have been discovered in the churchyard, and, while there is no clue as to who left them there or why, the valley they looked out upon would probably still look familiar to them today.

Carry on down the lane, with a stream coursing along a deep, fern-lined gulley on the right. At a T junction by Ashcombe Farm, turn right. As you continue down the valley, you can see the tower of Woolley church ahead on the right. *After 800m, turn right to follow a signpost for Woolley.* The lane drops steeply to a bridge over the Lam Brook, on the far side of which is Woolley Mill. This idyllic spot once had a sinister reputation, for in 1722 four Bristol merchants established gunpowder works here. It was clearly preferable to produce such a dangerous commodity in this isolated location rather than in a crowded city, although the locals may have been less than enthusiastic. A couple of years after the works opened, a night-time explosion left four workers dead and two seriously injured. Ten years later, another explosion killed a workman from Swainswick. Lessons seem to have been learned, however, for there were no further fatalities until the works closed in the early 19th century, and the mill went back to grinding corn.[1]

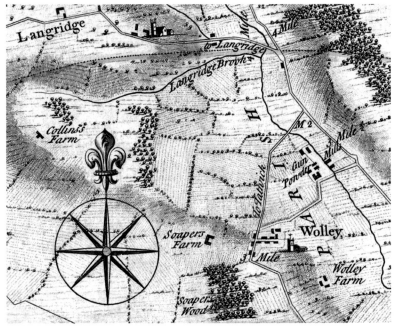

Woolley valley on Thorpe's map of 1742, showing the gunpowder mills

After climbing past Manor Farm, follow the lane as it bears left beside a wall with an ammonite. Carry on past a row of cottages, their walls studded with more ammonites, before turning left along Church Street to All Saints church, where plaques record Woolley's

1 See Buchanan, 'Bath's Forgotten Gunpowder History'.

status as one of the 'thankful villages' to which all the men who went to fight in World War One and World War Two returned. The church, designed by John Wood the Younger in 1761, is today regarded as a charming addition to this hidden village. At one time, though, it seems to have been regarded as such a monstrosity it is a wonder it escaped demolition.

The cupola of the Church of All Saints at Woolley seen above the roof of Manor Farm

Admittedly, it was admired enough in the 18th century. In the 1780s, Collinson described it as 'an elegant modern building with a handsome cupola'. Sixty years later, however, James Tunstall begged to 'differ from Collinson', describing it as 'an example of the want of taste in ecclesiastical architecture which prevailed during the last century, and early part of the present; it is debased Roman'. This was mild compared with the verdict of local historian REM Peach, who in 1890 wrote that it had 'scarcely a single merit to boast of, notwithstanding the eminence of the architect'. Three years later, the author of a guidebook to *Bath and Bristol and Forty Miles Round* declared that 'the tiny church is about 140 years old, and about as ugly as they could make them even at that period.' Mrs Wheatcroft, who compiled a book of walks around Bath in 1897, was more circumspect. 'But for its lovely surroundings the church might be considered uninteresting,' she wrote, 'in fact, I have heard people call it ugly; but to my mind, with the range of hills behind and the few cottages immediately in its vicinity, it has a peculiar charm of its own'. Indeed, one thing that all have agreed on is that the view across the valley to Swainswick, in whose church John Wood the

Younger lies interred alongside his father, is one of the most richly satisfying in an area not short of beautiful views.

It is here that you need to make a choice as to which route you want to follow back to Bath – an easier route along the lane and down a footpath into Larkhall, from where you can catch a bus back to the city centre; or a more challenging route, which involves a stiff climb through fields which will probably contain cattle, but leads to a series of spectacular views.

● *For the easier route: Head back up Church Street and turn left along the lane. After 1750m, when you come to a T junction, go straight ahead down a steep footpath. At the bottom, go down steps to where a brook runs into a culvert and bear left along a grassy strip between houses.* 🚌 *There is a bus stop across the road at the end, but, if you want to walk back to Bath, cross and carry on along the road ahead, passing two schools and turning right at the end. After 40m, when the road bears right, cross and carry straight on along Avondale Buildings. At the end, cross and carry on along Upper Lambridge Street, and bear right along the London Road at the end.*

Steps down to Larkhall

● *For the more scenic route, head back up Church Street and turn left along the lane. After 30m, turn right, following a footpath sign uphill* (ST748684). *Cross a stile beside a gate and carry on up a drive. Go through a KG on the left and carry on uphill through a field which may contain cattle. Follow a well-trodden path into a copse running along the top edge of the field.* The view eastward over the Woolley valley to Little Solsbury from here (which features opposite the title page) is especially fine, while the view southward across the field to Soper's Wood could have been designed to embody an 18th-century vision of pastoral bliss. *Carry on through a KG*, beyond which a bench commands a spectacular view of the valley.

Carry on up steps and through another KG, beyond which the public footpath has recently been rerouted to create a **cordon sanitaire** *around Charlcombe Grove Farm at the top of the field. Head uphill in the direction indicated by the waymark on the gate, through another field in which there may be cattle. As you climb, look for a gate silhouetted against the skyline to the right of a tree, and head towards it. As you approach it, follow a track up steps beside a fence to the right of the gate, before bearing left to go through it.*

THE WOOLLEY VALLEY RAILWAY

The Woolley valley is one of the most tranquil and unspoilt places in north east Somerset. It would have been very different, though, had the Midland Railway gone ahead with plans to drive a railway through it.

The Midland Railway Company's acquisition of the Bristol & Gloucester Railway in 1846 had given it a cross-country route from Leeds to Bristol. It had no intention of stopping there, however: its ultimate goal was the south coast. The company wasted no time in engaging Robert Stephenson to draw up plans for a line to Bath – the first link in a chain that would ultimately lead to the English Channel.

Stephenson decided that the line should leave the Bristol & Gloucester at Mangotsfield, five miles north of Bristol, from where it would travel south-west, passing north of Wick, before entering a 1446m tunnel under Tog Hill. It would emerge at Lower Hamswell and run downhill past Langridge, Woolley and Swainswick, before swinging south-east to cross the London Road just west of its junction with Gloucester Road. From here it would run through Grosvenor Gardens and Kensington Meadows, before crossing the river near the present Morrison's store, to terminate at a station in Bathwick Street, on the site now occupied by the fire station.

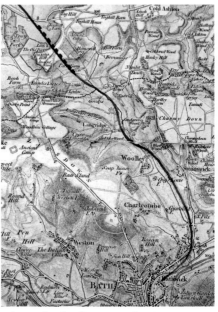

A map showing the proposed route

The company submitted a bill to parliament, but withdrew it after the second reading. The reasons for this are unclear. The branch was only 9.75 miles long and, apart from the tunnel, would have been relatively cheap to build. It passed through no major settlements and entered Bath through an area still largely undeveloped.

But railway companies were notoriously vulnerable to economic fluctuations in their early years. Perhaps the Midland was going through one of its periodic cashflow crises. It was empire building elsewhere as well – in 1846, it opened a line from Nottingham to Lincoln, two years later came a line from Leicester to Peterborough.

But perhaps the most likely explanation for the Midland's change of heart was because the Great Western had outmanoeuvred it. The only way south from Bathwick was up the Avon valley, but in 1846 the Great Western received parliamentary approval for a line from Bathampton to Bradford on Avon. With its route to the south effectively blocked, perhaps the Midland found the prospect of a line to Bath somewhat less enticing.

But the idea – and the dream of reaching the south coast – did not go away. In 1862, the Midland put forward another plan for a railway to Bath, branching off at Mangotsfield as before, but this time running south, through Oldland Common, Warmley and Bitton, before heading east along the Avon valley. The year is significant: it was in 1862 that two small railway companies – the Somerset Central and the Dorset Central – merged to form the Somerset & Dorset, with plans to create a through route between the Bristol and English Channels. The Midland's dream of a route to the south coast was back on the agenda.

The Midland line from Mangotsfield to Bath opened in 1869. Five years later, the Somerset & Dorset opened a 26-mile branch from Evercreech Junction to the Midland station at Bath. It cost so much to build that the company went bankrupt, and the line was taken over jointly by the Midland and the London & South Western Railways. The Midland had finally got its route to the south coast, although the line, which involved a 1672m-long tunnel under Combe Down and gradients far steeper than anything Stephenson had envisaged, posed operational difficulties until it closed in 1966.

Although the Midland line to Bath has, like the Somerset & Dorset, long gone, it has left a formidable legacy. When it was built, water meadows, gardens – and one of the finest cricket pitches in the country – disappeared under sidings, engine sheds and marshalling yards. In the wake of the railway came factories and warehouses. Today, all have gone. Part of the area is occupied by retail outlets and car parks; the Western Riverside development covers much of the rest.

If Stephenson's plan had gone ahead, what happened on the west side of the city could well have happened on the east. Kensington Meadows would be no more than a name on early 19th-century maps; the development that took place at Lower Weston may well have happened at Woolley and Swainswick; further up the valley, Langridge could have succumbed to late 19th-century developers, as Oldfield Park did after the Somerset & Dorset opened.

Although Stephenson's line would almost certainly have closed when the rail network was rationalised in the 1960s, it would have left us with a Woolley valley very different to the one we know today. We can only be grateful it never happened.

The well above Charlcombe Grove Farm, which, according to Thorpe's map of 1742, was once known as Soaper's Farm

A derelict and faintly sinister building

Carry on alongside a wall, passing what may well be the most spectacularly situated old well in Somerset. When you come to a 7-bar gate, go through a handgate beside it and carry on past the back of Charlcombe Grove Farm, with a derelict and faintly sinister 20th-century building to your right.

Continue along a drive and go through a handgate beside the gates at the end. Carry on in the same direction, passing an ornamental archway and a lodge with distinctive chimneys (ST742679). *Ahead, you will see a new housing estate built on a former MOD site. When you come to a lane, bear left, and after 100m bear right along a footpath, whose marker post has acquired a 20mph sign.* The view from here is remarkable, as it encompasses not only much of Bath's

A lodge with distinctive chimneys

southern escarpment, but also, far beyond it, the Mendips and the northern flank of Salisbury Plain, with the White Horse at Westbury visible on a clear day.

After 120m turn left across a slab stile and head downhill beside a hedgerow. The turreted tower you can see ahead is that of the Royal High School, dating from 1856. *After going through a KG, carry on beside the hedgerow. When you come to another KG go through it and turn right along Charlcombe Lane. After 100m, just past the gateposts of Charlcombe Manor, bear left along a rough lane which soon becomes a tree-lined path, with views across the valley to Little Solsbury. Before long, however, houses start to appear on the right and the path widens to a lane. When you come to a road, carry on in the same direction for another 350m. After passing Ragland Lane on the left, when the road curves down Marshfield Way, branch right to carry straight on along Summerfield Terrace* – pausing for a moment to take in a splendid view of the Avon valley, with Brown's Folly high on the slopes of Farleigh Down. *After 180m, follow the road as it bears right uphill, but, after another 60m, turn left past bollards along a path. At the end, carry straight on down a road, and, when this curves right after 140m, carry on along a footpath. Carry on in the same direction when it broadens to a road, and turn left at the bottom. After a few metres cross over and bear right down a footpath by a patch of grass, to follow the course of the old Lansdown Road. At the bottom, continue down Belvedere to return to the city centre.*

A footpath with a speed limit – and a superb view over Bath and beyond

Beyond Batheaston: Walk 7
Bannerdown & Little Solsbury

Distance: 12 miles;
  shorter options available by:
  catching a bus (3, X31) from Bath to Batheaston at the start;
  catching a bus (3, X31) from Batheaston to Bath at the end

Terrain: Some rough and rocky paths, as well as tracks across fields and possible muddy sections; sheep are likely to be encountered, as well as cows on Bannerdown and Little Solsbury.

Pubs and cafés: None beyond Batheaston

Map: OS Explorer 155 or AA Walker's Map 25

Opposite: Looking north from Little Solsbury to the caterpillar of beeches on Freezing Hill

In this walk, we head to Batheaston, before climbing to the twin peaks – or rather plateaus – of Bannerdown and Little Solsbury. The two summits are very different: Bannerdown is hemmed in by trees and offers little in the way of distant prospects, while Little Solsbury, encompassed by the ramparts of an iron age fort, commands the finest and most far-reaching views of any of the hills around Bath. Both, though, have been identified as the possible site of the Battle of Mount Badon, where – according to some accounts – King Arthur won a famous victory over Saxon forces.

Little Solsbury was also the setting for a more recent battle, when campaigners took to the treetops to try to stop a dual carriageway being built across its slopes in 1994. Although the road was eventually built, the groundswell of public support led to a drastic scaling-back of the government's road-building programme. Over 20 years later, however, the battle lines are being drawn again. Although plans to build a Park & Ride car park on the meadows below the hill were shelved in July 2017, following widespread protests, plans to build a link road from the dual carriageway and inflict further damage on this idyllic spot have been revived.

As well as taking in those meadows, the walk includes lost pleasure gardens, a secluded riverside path, green lanes (including one following the course of the Fosse Way), a house once famous as a 'nest of suffragettes' and a reed-filled nature reserve in a hidden valley.

Although there are no pubs, cafés or shops beyond Batheaston, there is plenty of climbing, so you are advised to carry water with you.

The full walk is 12 miles long, but there is the option of cutting it to 7 miles by starting and ending at Batheaston, which is linked to Bath by a frequent bus service.

From Kingston Parade, head east along the south side of the abbey and carry on into Orange Grove. Turn right past a row of shops, cross two sets of pedestrian lights, turn left and follow the balustrade round into Grand Parade. At the end, turn right across Pulteney Bridge, carry on along Argyle Street, and, when you reach Laura Place, turn left along Henrietta Street. After 100m, turn right through an archway into Henrietta Mews. Carry on along the road (or, if you prefer, bear left to walk through Henrietta Park), and, at the end of the park, continue past the Pulteney Arms along Daniel Street. At the end, turn left along Bathwick Street for 25m, cross at the pedestrian lights and carry straight on along an alleyway.

At the end, turn right along Powlett Road. A left turn at the end leads into Forester Road, built on the site of long-lost pleasure gardens called Villa Fields. At their heart stood Bathwick Villa, a grandiose

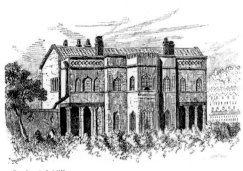

Bathwick Villa

and elaborate building dating from 1777. When it was demolished in 1897, some of its ornaments, including urns, pediments and a winged dragon, were used to embellish the houses on the left. *Take the first right along Forester Lane, turn left at the end along Beckford Gardens, continue along Hampton Row and cross the footbridge over the railway. Carry on along a footpath beside the railway, which after 100m joins a gravel path.* From here, there is a good view not only of the back of Grosvenor Place but also of Little Solsbury. A spring running under the path a little way along marks the boundary of Cremorne Pleasure Gardens, which stood on the right, and as you carry on down, you pass the ruins of the Folly public house (see pages 30-31).

At the bottom, turn left under the railway and then right through a kissing gate (KG) (ST763660). On your left is the end of a line of electricity pylons from Melksham to Bath erected, despite widespread protests, in 1943. This is as far as they got because extending them any further westward would have been considered, even then, too visually intrusive. Today, the case for burying the 2.5 mile stretch of cables from the Wiltshire border to the outskirts of Bath would seem overwhelming, were it not for the resolution of some local politicians and lobbyists to develop further the fields through our walk now lies.[1]

Carry straight on across the field, and, after going through a gateway, follow a track – parts of which may be waterlogged – towards the road bridges you can see in the distance. After following a metalled path under the four bridges (a dual carriageway and two slip roads) carry straight on across a field. After crossing a pair of stiles, continue along a drive beside a field which local councillors recently earmarked for an 800-1200 space Park & Ride car park, only to have their offer to buy it turned down by the farmer who owns it.

1 In 2014, the government announced that £500m would be made available to bury hundreds of miles of cables strung on pylons through Areas of Outstanding Natural Beauty (AONBs). It is unclear whether any of this money could be use to bury the cables on Bathampton Meadows – surrounded as they are by the Cotswolds AONB – but, as one of the arguments used by those pushing for the development of the meadows is that the view is already marred by pylons, it is hardly to be expected they would want to explore the possibility.

When you come to a road, cross and go through a gate opposite to follow a gravel track alongside a meadow. This meadow is where councillors opted to build their car park after their initial plan was thwarted. The impact such a move would have had is apparent if you look around to see the places it would have been visible from – not just Claverton, Bathampton and Farleigh Downs, and Little Solsbury, but also the villages of Batheaston, Bathford and Bathampton. To say that it would have compromised Bath's World Heritage setting seems something of an understatement. The plan was shelved in July 2017, following a long and bitter campaign by local residents, and after Highways England raised concerns over access. However, plans to build a link road from the dual carriageway to the A36, with potentially even graver environmental consequences, are still being pursued.

When the track curves right, turn left across a small footbridge (ST775670)*, follow a track under the road and carry on through the car park of Bathampton Mill.* After the mill was destroyed by fire in 1895, tea gardens opened in its grounds. In the 1960s, part of the old building was converted to a nightclub called the Keel Club, whose fame spread far and wide, before it closed and became a restaurant in the 1970s. *Turn left along the road. After crossing the toll bridge,* opened in 1870 to replace a ferry, *bear right down a drive.* To your left, through the gates of Avondale House, can be seen the tower of the old Avondale Brewery, now converted to offices.

Head along a footpath to the left of the gates to the Old Mill Hotel, which stands on the site of a mill destroyed by fire in 1909. *Carry on, ignoring a footpath branching left, to enjoy a delightful riverside walk,* with views across to Bathampton Meadows. After 500m, you also have a surprise glimpse of one of Batheaston's grandest buildings. Batheaston House, with its gardens running down to the river, was built in 1712 by Henry Walters, on the foundations of an earlier house which he inherited and demolished. His family's wealth came from the clothing trade, and he was not only the most powerful

Along the riverside path

man in Batheaston, but also became high sheriff for Somerset.

Just before the footbridge, turn left past a gateway into what was once part of Batheaston House's gardens. Now owned by the council, an 18th-century shell niche and seat can still be seen

Batheaston House

on the other side of the wall. *Head up to the road, turn right to cross at the pedestrian lights and carry on to the mini-roundabout, before taking the second left up Fosse Lane.*

🚌 *If travelling to Batheaston by bus, get off at Stambridge, just past the George & Dragon and White Lion pubs. From the bus stop, head back to the mini roundabout and head north up Fosse Lane.*

Fiveway House, on the corner of Fosse Lane, dates from the late 18th century, but may incorporate an earlier building. It was used by the Poor Law Guardians as a home for boys in the early 20th century, and is also believed to have been a beerhouse around 1860. It has recently been restored after years of neglect.

Climbing the Fosse

Fosse Lane, as its name suggests, follows the course of the Roman Fosse Way. The houses lining it become ever grander until, as Bannerdown Drive curves off to the right, it carries on up a holloway (ST783678). This, despite all appearances to the contrary, is still the Roman road, little changed from 1791, when the Rev John Collinson wrote that 'the Fosse here is deep, narrow, and overhung with hedges'. He went on to explain that this was 'a circumstance, which, in many cases, the Romans could not avoid; sometimes being under the necessity of humouring the ground, and at other times of

BANNERDOWN & THE BATTLE OF MOUNT BADON

The Batheaston Freeholders Association has managed Bannerdown, along with Little Solsbury, since 1719. These areas of limestone grassland are home to a variety of rare meadow flowers, while Bannerdown is fringed by extensive former quarry workings, which form a network of wildlife-rich habitats.

Unlike Little Solsbury, with its iron age ramparts, however, Bannerdown appears to have little in the way of historic interest. Even the Roman road that crossed it has virtually disappeared. Bannerdown has a long and distinguished history of human occupation, however. Mesolithic flints have been found here, and in the 17th century John Aubrey made a sketch – now in Oxford's Bodleian Library – of a

'sepulchre' on Bannerdown, which appears to have been a long barrow. No trace of it survives, but it has been suggested that the three large stones used in 1858 to create a 'cromlech' over the Three Shires Stone beside the Fosse Way less than a mile  to the north came from this barrow. Vestigial traces of pre-Roman or Romano-British earthworks, including field boundaries and a possible camp, have also been discovered here.

For many, though, Bannerdown's main interest lies in its possible identification as the site of the Battle of Mons Badonicus or Mount Badon, at which Romano-British forces – possibly led by King Arthur – repelled an Anglo-Saxon advance in the late 5th or early 6th century. The earliest account of the battle was written by the chronicler Gildas around AD540. He called it 'the siege of Mount Badon' [*obsessio montis Badonici*], and claimed that it took place in the year of his birth, which is thought to have been around AD496. He identified the leader of the Romano-British forces not as Arthur, however, but as Ambrosius Aurelianus. The Venerable Bede, writing in AD731, gave a similar account of what he called 'the siege of Mount Badon'. Not until the early 9th century, when a Welsh monk called Nennius wrote his *Historium Britonum*, did the name of Arthur appear for the first time. According to Nennius, in 'the battle on Mount Badon [*bellum in monte Badonis*] ... 960 men fell in one day from a single charge of Arthur's, and no one laid them low save he alone'.

It is not just the question of who led the Romano-British forces that is in dispute; the location of the battle has long been a source of conjecture. John Wood believed it took place on Lansdown, while others have suggested Hampton Down and Little Solsbury as possible sites. More distant locations – in Wiltshire, Dorset, Somerset, Wales and Scotland –

have also been suggested. John Aubrey, however, who grew up eight miles away at Easton Piercy in Wiltshire, wrote that, 'on Bannes-downe, above Ben-Easton near Bathe, where a battle of king Arthur was fought, are great stones scattered in the same manner as they are on Durnham-downe, about Bristow [Bristol], which was assuredly the work of an earthquake, when these great cracks and vallies were made.'

Bannerdown has two things in its favour: the similarity between its name and that of Badon (although this also applies to two other candidates – Badbury Rings in Dorset and Lidding-ton Castle near Bad-bury in Wiltshire), and the Roman road running across it. The Fosse Way would have been a natural route for an invading army to take through hostile territory, and Bannerdown would have been the last place the Romano-British would have had a realistic chance of stopping the invaders before they sped downhill towards the city below, control of which was key to further incursions beyond the Avon.

Bannerdown in late autumn, winter and early spring

It is also worth mentioning that the Roman road from Bath to London was once known as the Via Badonica. This name was not given to it by the Romans, but was in use by the early 18th century. Unfortunately, all this proves is that whoever decided to give it this name did so because he believed that the battle was fought somewhere along its course.

making use of those hollows which nature herself had formed therein by torrents from the hills.'

Carry on up the Fosse Way, and, after passing an information board for Bannerdown Common, continue alongside the wall on your right. When you come to a gate with waymarks, go through it and follow a bridleway sign up a broad and muddy track on the left. When you see a bench up ahead, follow a footpath sign towards it, and carry on up a track. When the ground levels out, take a track bearing left ahead. As you carry on in the same direction, old quarries can be seen to left and right, before Bannerdown opens out before you. Here, little trace of the Roman road survives, but old maps show it running diagonally across to the far corner of the field, where it is joined by the modern road, which takes a somewhat gentler and more circuitous course uphill.

Follow a track along the left-hand side of the field, and go through a handgate on the left at the end (ST792689). *Follow a footpath diagonally downhill into woods, and, when you come to a farm track, carry on in the same direction along it. When you come to a lane (known as Steway Lane) cross and follow a footpath sign along a green holloway running straight downhill.*

After 400m, the holloway curves right and gets rougher before coming to an abrupt end, at which point you have to go through a handgate on the right and carry on across the top of a field, with a fence on your right. After going through a gap into the next field, bear left downhill alongside the hedge. At the bottom left-hand corner of

The monks' causeway at Upper Northend Farm

the field, cross a footbridge and carry straight on uphill. Go through a gate at the top and turn left along a lane past Upper Northend Farm, in front of which can be seen a causeway built by the monks of Bath Abbey (ST782691). It ran to the monastic grange at St Catherine's, and, at a time when lanes such as this were often quagmires in the rainy season, helped those who came this way to keep their feet dry.

Carry on past the turning for Hollies Lane, and, 250m further on, you come to Eagle House, so called because of the dodo-like eagle atop its pediment. The architect John Wood the Younger lived here in his later years, and in the early 20th century, when it was the home of the Blathwayt family, it became famous as a 'nest of suffragettes'.

Take the next right up Eagle Road, through an estate built on the site of an arboretum where suffragettes who stayed at Eagle House planted over 60 trees. The only tree to survive is an Austrian Pine, now over a century old, which can be seen up rising up behind the house on the corner of Eagle Park. *At the top of Eagle Road, turn right along Seven Acres Lane and follow it as curves left uphill. After climbing steadily, the lane drops down to Chilcombe Bottom, where a reservoir built in 1848 is now a nature reserve. Go through a gate behind the lock-up-style valve house and bear right to follow a path through the reserve. Go through*

Above: Eagle House

Below: An Austrian Pine, sole survivor of the suffragette arboretum

Bottom: The valve house at Chilcombe Bottom

EAGLE HOUSE

Despite Peter Gabriel's assurances, visitors to Little Solsbury are unlikely to see an eagle flying out of the night as they gaze from its ramparts. Compensation of a sort, though, comes in the form of a somewhat unconvincing carving of an eagle on a house nestling under Little Solsbury's eastern slopes. Eagle House dates from the mid to late 17th century, and, like many of Batheaston's grand houses, was originally gabled and built of rubble stone. When the south side was remodelled in 1724, ashlar stone was used to fill in the space between its three gables and create a parapet. The central window on the first floor was also replaced by a Venetian window with blind outer lights. Beneath it was inserted an Ionic doorcase with heavily-banded columns. All this was in the latest style, as though the owner – or the builder he employed – had seen the designs in

a pattern book and wanted to try them out. Spectacular though the effect is, you can clearly see where the spaces between the gables were filled in, while the central features do not harmonise with the rest of the façade.

We know it was remodelled in 1724 because the date – along with the initials SC – appears on the wall. SC was probably Samuel Clement, who died in 1728 and was buried in Batheaston church. In 1729 – four years after the south side had been remodelled, and a year after Samuel Clement's death – it was the turn of the east side. This remodelling, which included the aforementioned eagle, was even more flamboyant, and, if the identification of SC as Samuel Clement is correct, we can perhaps see this as the expression of the new owner's desire to make his mark on the house. It could well have been his son, although there is another contender – no less a personage than the architect John Wood.

The legend that John Wood owned and remodelled Eagle House is of long standing, and, although it has been debunked, is still very much current. It even makes an appearance in Historic England's listing designation for the building. As long ago as 1969, however, a local historian called Beatrice Dobbie disproved the claim that John Wood lived in the house, although she was prepared to accept that he may have remodelled the east front. Tim Mowl and Brian Earnshaw, in their 1988 study of John Wood, made no bones about refuting that story as well:

> No myth has done more to obscure his character than the fiction that in 1729 he bought Eagle House in Batheaston, altered it to his taste and settled there in rural seclusion. A line in Collinson's *History of Somerset*, 1791, stating that a house in the village 'was the residence of the late ingenious architect John Wood' may have begun the legend. The facts are that a late 17th-century house on the site was altered in 1724, while Wood was still in London, and in 1729 a front was added to the road by an anonymous mason in a homely but competent West Country baroque. At a later stage a porch was added with blocked columns, a style current around the 1730s but not one which Wood affected for doorways. In 1773, long after Wood's death, his son John was living in the house and actually died there.

So who did the work on Eagle House? One contender is an architect called Thomas Greenway, who designed other buildings in a similar style. Among them was a house for Beau Nash on the Sawclose in Bath, whose doorway is flanked by eagles reminiscent of the one on Eagle House. For the moment, however, this must remain speculation.

Eagle House has an even more remarkable claim to fame, however. In 1882, Lieutenant Colonel Linley Blathwayt, whose father had been Rector of Langridge, returned home from India and bought Eagle House. At some time during the late 18th or early 19th century, a single-storey extension had been built at the west end of the south front. In 1907-8, Lt Col Blathwayt engaged a local architect called Mowbray Green to rebuild it as a two-storey extension.

One reason he may have needed more space was his wife and daughter's increasing involvement with the women's suffrage movement. His daughter Mary was not only a prominent local campaigner and organiser, but invited many leading suffragettes to convalesce at Eagle House after they had been on hunger strike in prison. Between 1909 and 1912, over 60 suffragettes stayed at Eagle House, each of whom planted a tree in a nearby field. A plaque was placed by each tree to record the event and the field became known as Annie's Arboretum, after the suffragette Annie Kenney, who was a frequent visitor. After the Blathwayt family sold Eagle House in 1962, however, the trees were bulldozed, along with many of the plaques, to make way for a housing estate. Only one tree survived – a lofty Austrian Pine, planted by Rose Lamartine Yates on 30 October 1909 after a month's imprisonment in Holloway Gaol.

a gate at the end, turn right and carry on up the valley along a green lane between high hedges. After going through a handgate, carry on along the lane, with Little Solsbury up to your left.

After 350m, go through a six-bar gate on the left and follow a track heading diagonally up to the right past a waymark post (ST763684). *After the track starts to climb steeply, continue up steps and go through a KG at the top.*

Turn left alongside the hedge, and carry on through a KG to follow a path between hedges. After re-emerging into the open, carry on uphill, and, after going through another KG, head up through the ramparts of Little Solsbury, across ground disturbed by quarrying. To your right, you will see a mizmaze cut in 1994 by campaigners trying to stop the construction of the dual carriageway below the hill.

Once within the ramparts, bear left along the perimeter. Beneath your feet survive remnants of the dry stone wall which lined the ramparts, while rocky outcrops can be seen on the slopes below. The view northward is bounded by Charmy Down, some 20m higher than Little Solsbury. Geologists have suggested that Little Solsbury once formed part of Charmy Down, but was separated from it by a major landslip, creating the valley of Chilcombe Bottom.[1] Ahead though, the views extend to the Marlborough Downs, some 17 miles away, rearing up like a distant coastline espied across leagues of ocean. At their southern end is Roundway Down, whose wooded slopes drop down to Devizes. It was on Roundway, eight days after the Battle of Lansdown, that Royalist troops faced Waller's Parliamentary forces once again. This time, the Parliamentarians were roundly defeated, the victorious Royalists pursuing them to the edge of the escarpment, where many tumbled headlong to their deaths.

Scanning north from Roundway Down, past two large beech hangers, you should, on a clear day, be able to make out the radio masts on Morgan's Hill, while further north is the 37m-high Lansdowne Monument, built in 1845 by the Marquis of Lansdowne above the village of Cherhill.

As you ***continue along the eastern ramparts***, Batheaston lies below you, although from here most of the old village is hidden by trees. The Little Solsbury plateau is roughly triangular and its southern extremity commands a superb panorama, with Bathampton and Farleigh Downs framing the Limpley Stoke Valley, and the Westbury White Horse in the distance.

As you ***continue along the ramparts***, the caterpillar of trees on Freezing Hill comes into view to the north, while below, through what

---

1 See Oswin and Buettner, *Little Solsbury Hill Camp*, p. 35: Hobbs & Jenkins, *Bath's 'foundered strata'*, p.19.

THE WHITE HORSE AND THE CATERPILLAR

There are two landmarks which, although not visited in the course of these walks, are visible from an astonishing number of viewpoints, and, as they kept on appearing on the horizon, it seemed only fitting to say something about them.

The first is the White Horse above Westbury in Wiltshire. Although 14 miles from Bath, this is visible from Lansdown and Little Solsbury as well as from much of the high ground south and east of the city. It is believed to have been created in the late 17th century to commemorate King Alfred's victory over the Danes at the Battle of Ethandun. Like other white horses, it was made by cutting into the chalk and had to be maintained by frequent scouring. It was recut and

The Westbury White Horse in 1887

reprofiled in 1778 and 1873, and in the 1950s was covered in concrete from the nearby concrete works. The concrete was renewed in 1995 and has since been painted and restored.

The second landmark is the row of beech trees – known as the caterpillar – on Freezing Hill (ST722713), half a mile north of the Lansdown Monument. It stands on the boundary between the parishes

The Freezing Hill Caterpillar

of Cold Ashton and Doynton and, at its western end, meets a bank and ditch, 540m long, which is referred to as an 'eald dic' (old dyke) in a Saxon charter and may date from the iron age. The age and significance of the row of trees is unknown, although a late 19th-century OS map indicates that at one time it extended further east, meeting Freezing Hill Lane at its junction with the drive to Tracy Cottage Farm. Among those who have been captivated by this iconic feature is the artist Nick Cudworth, whose studio is on London Street in Bath. He has produced a series of paintings showing it from a range of viewpoints and at different seasons. More on the caterpillar can be found at *bathnewseum.com/tag/freezing-hill* and *www.nickcudworth.co.uk*.

seems like a near permanent haze, lies the city of Bath. At first glance, modern buildings seem to predominate, although the most immediately recognisable landmark is St Saviour's church in Larkhall, at the foot of the hill. In the distance, though, you should also be able to make out the Abbey tower, half-hidden by the Empire Hotel. You can also see Bath's only tower block, twelve-storey Berkeley House on Snow Hill, with the

An October sunset from Little Solsbury

Rocky outcrops below the ramparts

long sweep of the Paragon behind it, while to the right is the distinctive curve of Camden Crescent, dropping steeply away at the far end.

When you reach a trig point (188m above sea level), head down to the bench you can see below you, and bear right to follow a rough and muddy track, through humps and bumps, gradually downhill. The track is unclear in places, but, if you carry on in the same direction, you will find it broadening and curving more steeply down to a KG by a seven-bar gate.

Go through the KG and bear left alongside the hedgerow. After going through another KG at the end of the field, turn right along a lane for 35m and then left along a footpath (ST765675). *When you come to another lane, continue along a footpath a few metres over to the left.*

Carry straight on past the backs of buildings to emerge on Bailbrook Lane. Turn left past a row of cottages, with an old tin church, dating from 1892, at the end. Ahead, a row of lofty poplars, rustling in the breeze, masks the sound of the nearby dual carriageway.

Bailbrook's old tin church

The Avon valley from above Batheaston, known as Arno's Vale in the 18th century

After 250m turn left up a drive with a public footpath sign and follow it as it curves past the back of a house. Carry on through a wooden KG and follow a track across a field. From here you have a view over one of the finest stretches of the Avon valley. On a sultry summer's day,

An 18th-century view of the Avon valley at Batheaston, with Bailbrook House on the left and Bannerdown to the right

there is an Italianate quality to the view, which struck 18th-century visitors to Bath, who, according to Collinson, compared it to that of the Arno near Florence:

> Batheaston is bounded and divided from Bath Hampton by the river Avon, which, fringed with willows, forms an easy bend through a range of fine rich meads, called Arno's-Vale ... The houses standing along the turnpike-road overlook this beautiful valley, with the village of Hampton, embosomed in trees on the opposite banks of the Avon, and overhung by the lofty ridge of Hampton-down, whereon plantations of firs, and patches of rugged rocks, are contrasted with each other.

Despite everything those impervious to its charms have done – or tried to do – to this glorious valley, his description still holds true today.

Go through another KG which leads across a ha-ha. Continue through two more KGs, carry on along a narrow, overgrown path (ignoring another KG on the left), follow steep steps downhill and turn right along a lane (ST776676). *After 35m, go through a KG on the left with a footpath sign. Head straight downhill and follow steps down to a gated footbridge, with Batheaston church ahead. Carry on along to another KG, and a little further on follow steps down to the road and turn right. After passing the bottom of Solsbury Lane, follow the raised pavement on the right called The Batch, carry on along a lane at the end, and cross over when you reach the main road.*

🚌 *If you want to take a bus back to the city centre, you can catch it here.*

Otherwise, carry on, and, just past the end of the 20mph section (opposite the entrance to Tower House), turn left down a footpath. Turn right at the T junction at the bottom, and, after passing the Old Mill Hotel, carry on through a tunnel under the road. Continue through a wooded area for 50m before emerging in an overgrown meadow. If you wish, before carrying on, you can bear left to see where the ferry once ran across to Bathampton Mill. *Head across the meadow, continue along a tree-shaded path and past an archery ground, and, after*

Through woodland near the tollbridge

passing a venerable willow, on emerging in a rugby ground, bear left alongside the hedge (ST771668). *Bear right to carry on alongside the river, and, at the end of the field, carry on along a narrow track for 50m.*

When you come to a tarmac path, turn left. Follow the path under the dual carriageway and up to the London Road, where a left turn will take you back to the city centre. However, the London Road, although lined with some of Bath's most attractive Georgian buildings, is busy and congested, so, if you want a break from all that air pollution, turn left, after 300m, along Grosvenor Bridge Road. At the end, turn right and carry on through a gate, where you can either head straight across Kensington Meadows or divert left to walk alongside the river, before heading up through a supermarket car park and continuing back into the city centre along the London Road and Walcot Street.

Bathampton Mill and the site of the ferry crossing c1890

Little Solsbury & the Battle of the Bypass

The ramparts on Little Solsbury date from the Iron Age, and the land within them was occupied as a camp or hillfort from around 300BC to 100BC. Alone among the hills surrounding Bath, Little Solsbury commands views in every direction, a distinction it shares with Kelston Round Hill, three and a half miles to the west. The views from Little Solsbury, though, are perhaps even more spectacular. Even so, it takes a leap of the imagination to comprehend what they would have been like before the modern age, with its roads and urban sprawl, when the only sounds would have been those of the wind, of sheep cropping the turf and of skylarks high above. Or of what it would have been like, when the camp was occupied, looking out over the valley robed in moonlight. On moonless nights, the darkness would have been broken only by the pinprick, flickering gleams of fires in camps ringing the horizon, and the only sounds would have been those of the birds and animals of the night, the hunters and the hunted.

Beyond that, history shelves off into myth. Little Solsbury is another of the candidates for the site of the Battle of Mount Badon – and here, unlike Bannerdown, that battle would have been very much in the nature of a siege. Writing in 1791, the Rev John Collinson also recorded the legend that Bladud built a temple dedicated to Apollo here. More prosaically, he added that, in his day, the land within the ramparts was an 'arable field' yielding 'fine crops of barley'.

Little Solsbury's current fame, though, was assured when Peter Gabriel released *Solsbury Hill* in 1977, describing a mystical moment when 'time stood still' as he climbed its slopes. Ironically, this is one of Jeremy Clarkson's Desert Island Discs – ironically because it was the Conservative government's road-building programme that propelled Little Solsbury to national attention. The question of whether King Arthur fought the Saxons here may be a matter of conjecture; there was nothing illusory about the battle fought on Little Solsbury in 1994.

This was the first of the great anti-road building protests of the 1990s. Spurred into action by the imminent destruction of a landscape little changed for millennia, the group of activists who took to the trees in the path of the diggers in March 1994 soon had a groundswell of local and national feeling behind them, and in mid-May a weekend of action saw 1,200 people march on Little Solsbury.

Opposite: The mizmaze cut by campaigners in 1994 with the bypass beyond

The response of the authorities was draconian, with police and security forces using brute force to clear the campaigners out of their way, a tactic which backfired spectacularly. Some of the confrontations were captured by photographer Adrian Arbib. When the photographs were published, showing the campaigners responding with dignity to intimidation and violence, it was plain for all to see that the campaigners, far from being the feckless rabble the authorities had portrayed them as, were idealists fighting for a cause – and a cause, moreover, with which a growing number of people were in sympathy. These were individuals undergoing hardship, abuse and provocation not for personal gain, but to try to save the environment and preserve a nationally important heritage site for future generations. The photographs also revealed the lengths to which those intimidating them were prepared to go.[1]

Ultimately, the battle was lost and the road was built, but the campaigners, by raising awareness of the implications of the government's road-building programme, successfully derailed around 300 other schemes. One lasting reminder of the campaign is the mizmaze cut in the turf below Little Solsbury's ramparts by the campaigners. It commands a view up the Swainswick valley, with the caterpillar of trees at Freezing Hill on the horizon, a view now blighted by the dual carriageway slicing through it. Having been maintained and recut over the years, most recently in 2016, the mizmaze is still in remarkably good shape.

Surveying the scene from Little Solsbury today, the legacy of the government's intransigence is only too apparent. Over 20 years on, a similar intransigence has raised its head once more. In July 2017, local councillors decided – at least for the time being – not to pursue plans, which had already cost over £3M, to build a Park & Ride car park on the riverside meadows below the hill. Opponents of the scheme, along with many independent experts, pointed out that it would have had little or no impact on Bath's traffic problems, but would be a hugely expensive and environmentally devastating white elephant. A series of demonstrations, larger than any Bath had seen for years, were staged in the run-up to the council's U-turn; had work got under way the campaign would undoubtedly have escalated. The inheritors of the spirit of 1994 – and no doubt some of the original campaigners – would not have let the wanton destruction of heritage and environment go unchallenged.

An even more insidious threat has taken its place, however. The Batheaston bypass was originally planned as a link in a superhighway linking Southampton to the M4. With plans to extend it shelved, Bath was left with what George Monbiot described in 2009 as 'a high-spec

1 The photographs can be viewed at www.solsburyhill.org.uk, which includes much more about the campaign.

dual carriageway to nowhere'.[1] He added that 'building our way out of congestion and pollution is now a discredited idea, and for this the campaigners of Solsbury Hill can claim some responsibility'.

Despite this, proposals to resurrect the original plan and link the bypass with the A36 Warminster Road have rumbled on for years. Although only short, this new road would have a massive impact, and not only on the immediate area. Linking the A46 and the A36 would effectively make two narrow, winding and geologically unstable roads on the sides of steep valleys part of a major trunk route. Although the A46 and A36 are currently used as a through route by HGVs and other vehicles, many drivers are deterred from using the route because they either have to drive through Bath or, if their vehicle is small enough, use the single-carriageway tollbridge at Batheaston. Promoting increased usage of roads little changed, in terms of width or profile, since stagecoach days, and already overburdened by traffic, seems an act of folly. The A36, in particular, is so prone to slippage and subsidence that it has had to be closed for lengthy periods in recent years to shore it up, work that, by the nature of the terrain it runs through, can never provide a long-term solution.

George Monbiot's belief that building our way out of congestion and pollution was a discredited idea now seems to have been over-optimistic. When he returned to the subject of the bypass protest in May 2017, he made no bones about the enormity of the challenges facing us today:

> I remember being struck by the thought – when lying with a group of dreadlocked anarchists at the foot of an iron age hill fort, in the path of an earth mover commissioned by John Major's government – that we were the conservatives and they were the destructives. We were seeking to defend the fabric of the nation while they, with their road schemes joining the dots between scheduled ancient monuments, chalk downlands, water meadows and woodlands, were trying to pulp it. They claimed to be patriots, but we loved this country more than they did ... I find it hard to see how anyone can love people without also loving the living world that gave rise to us, or can love our civilisation without loving what remains of those that came before.[2]

The battle lines are drawn; only history will tell whether the fight to save this precious part of our inheritance will succeed. For the sake of future generations, though, we can only hope that it does.

To find out more about the threat of an A36-A46 link road, visit www. a36a46linkroadfacts.org.uk; for information on the threat to Bathampton Meadows, visit bathamptonmeadowsalliance.org.uk.

1 *Guardian*, 11 February 2009
2 *Guardian*, 3 May 2017

Beyond Batheaston: Walk 8
St Catherine's Valley, Marshfield &
Charmy Down

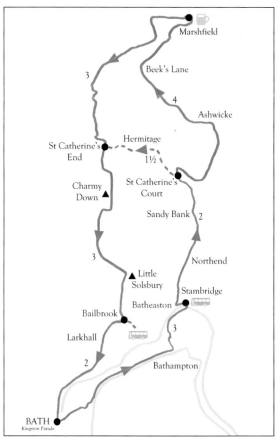

Distance: 17 miles; shorter options available by:
  catching a bus (3, X31) from Bath to Batheaston at the start;
  following an alternative route between St Catherine's Court and
    St Catherine's End;
  catching a bus (3, X31) from Batheaston to Bath at the end

Opposite: Halldoor Lane, Marshfield

(Note: There are no suitable buses from Marshfield to Bath; should you wish to return from Marshfield by public transport, the only option is to catch an infrequent bus to Bristol and take a bus or train back to Bath from there.)

Terrain: Lanes or green lanes, along with field tracks, and some steep and possibly muddy sections; sheep and cattle are likely to be encountered at several points

Pubs and cafés:

Catherine Wheel, Marshfield; open all day; lunch served 12-2 Mon-Fri, 12-3 Sat & Sun (www.thecatherinewheel.co.uk; 01225 892220)

Lord Nelson, Marshfield; lunch served 12-2 Mon-Sat, 12-3 Sun (www.lordnelsonatmarshfield.com; 01225 891820)

Sweetapples Teashop, Marshfield; open daily to 4pm (01225 891657)

Map: OS Explorer 155 or AA Walker's Map 25

This walk heads northwards into the Cotswolds to visit Marshfield, once one of Gloucestershire's most prosperous towns, but now, as if frozen in time, a place that history has passed by. To get there, we leave Bath along the towpath of the Kennet & Avon Canal, before crossing the meadows to Batheaston, where 17th-century weavers' cottages stand beside grand mill-owners' houses. Heading north, we follow a medieval causeway into a hidden valley hailed in old guidebooks as one of the most scenic in England.

At the heart of the valley lies St Catherine's Court, once a monastic grange, and the point where we strike out north into Gloucestershire to climb the southern flank of the Cotswolds and follow green lanes to Marshfield, where there are inns and a café to fortify you for the walk back.

Leaving Marshfield, we drop down from the Cotswold edge to follow the headwaters of St Catherine's Brook, before climbing to the bleak fastness of Charmy Down, where evidence of Neolithic settlement, preserved for millennia, was obliterated to create the World War Two airfield whose ruins now litter the site. From there, another valley and a final climb lead to the ramparts of Little Solsbury, before we head back down through Bailbrook to Bath.

Such at any rate, is the full walk, which runs to 17 miles – but there are shorter options. As with the previous walk, you can catch a bus to and from Batheaston, cutting 5 miles off the total. You can also omit the northern section of the walk, and, instead of heading north to Marshfield, continue along St Catherine's Valley before climbing to Charmy Down and heading back to Bath from there – still a very satisfying walk, and clocking in at just 11½ miles (or 6½ miles if you catch the bus to and from Batheaston).

One final point: Although much of the walk is through fields and along green lanes, the section through St Catherine's Valley keeps to lanes used by vehicles, even though footpaths through fields run parallel for much of the way. There are three reasons for this: first, the paths through the valley often range from the very muddy to the impassable; second, cows graze many of the fields and tend to congregate by muddy gateways, making it difficult to get through; third, using paths would mean missing out on a succession of fascinating buildings. The lanes are, admittedly, narrow, but see relatively little traffic, and are well used by walkers. Indeed, at least as far as St Catherine there are signs giving pedestrians priority. Should you choose, however, to use the footpaths, they are clearly marked on maps.

From Kingston Parade, head east along the south side of the abbey and carry on into Orange Grove. Turn right past a row of shops, cross two sets of pedestrian lights, turn left and follow the balustrade round into Grand Parade. At the end, turn right across Pulteney Bridge, carry on along Argyle Street and Great Pulteney Street, and, after crossing the pedestrian lights at the end, go into Sydney Gardens. Follow the broad path up through the gardens and, after crossing the railway, head up to a gate to the right of the bridge over the canal. After going through it, bear left along the towpath.

Carry on for 1½ miles, and, when you reach the George Inn, head down steps to the road and head north along it, passing Bathampton church on your right. After crossing the railway, continue over the dual carriageway, and, 100m further on, bear right through a gate (ST776667) *to follow a gravel track* beside meadows until recently earmarked for a Park & Ride car park (see pages 75-6 & 92).

Follow the track as it curves right alongside the River Avon. After crossing a footbridge over the river, head up to the road and turn left.

🚌 *If you have caught a bus to Batheaston, get off at Stambridge (just past the mini-roundabout beyond the George & Dragon and White Lion pubs at the far end of the village). Cross at the traffic island and head back along the main road in the direction of Bath.*

After passing a high wall, screening Batheaston House, on the left, you pass the old 17th-century Manor House at No 288. Like most of Batheaston's older buildings it is of rubble stone, rather than the smooth ashlar used in Bath's Georgian buildings. Ashlar was little used before the mid-18th century because it was prohibitively expensive. Even so, the presence of so many stone buildings – such as the three cottages beyond the Manor House (Nos 286-282) – indicates not only a supply of good quality local stone but also the relative affluence of Batheaston at the time.

The juxtaposition of grand houses with rows of cottages, which typifies the older part of the village, is a legacy of the way the local cloth industry operated. Merchants bought wool, sorted and dyed it, then sent it out to be carded in workshops. It then went to weavers who made it into cloth, before it was put through a fulling mill. Finally, it was dressed or finished by having its nap raised by teasels. Unlike weavers' cottages in other parts of the country, those in Batheaston are not characterised by large windows flooding workshops on the upper storeys with light. Because the machinery used was too large to be housed upstairs, it was accommodated in single-storey extensions at the back, which are still a feature of many of Batheaston's cottages today.[1]

A little further along, No 264 may date from the 16th century, and the pitch of its roof suggests it was originally thatched. Next door, a 19th-century ghost sign for a baker's recalls long-forgotten products such as corn bran, gurgeons and barley meal.

Cross at the pedestrian lights to one of Batheaston's most striking buildings, built in the 18th century when ashlar stone was more readily available. The empty space to the right of it is one of the saddest sights in Batheaston, for this is where the 17th-century Lamb Inn stood. It closed in 1962 and, after it was demolished, three houses were built on land at the back.

Turn right along the Batch, which follows the course of a causeway built by the prior of Bath Abbey to make it easier to get to and from the abbey grange at St Catherine. *When the lane curves downhill, carry on along a narrow path lined with old cottages. Follow it as it curves left and carry on along a road.*

Dolphin House, a little further along, may seem rather undistinguished. That is because you are looking at the back. You cannot see the other side – unless of course you check into the B&B – but, if you could, you would find not only gardens running down to St Catherine's Brook, but also a well-proportioned and imposing Georgian façade.

After passing the church, built in the 12th century, but rebuilt in the 15th and again in the 19th, you come to Pine House, on the right, dating from 1672. Once again, it is the back of the building you are looking at. When it was advertised to let in the *Gloucester Journal* on 23

---

1 For more on Batheaston's history see Dobbie, *Batheaston: An English Rural Community*

January 1739, it was described as 'very convenient for a Clothier, and ... a Place long-accustomed in that Way of Trade'. Adjoining the house were a dyehouse and mill, and, although the mill was demolished in the 1870s, the dyehouse survives. If you look at the north wing of the house, abutting the road, you will see what look like a pair of garage doors. This was the entrance to a lane leading to a bridge over the brook, on the far side of which was the mill. The dyehouse stands beside the lane, which was a public right of way until 1829, when the owner of Pine House applied to have it closed off as 'a useless footway'.

As you continue along the road, notice the blocked archway in the churchyard wall, which once led to the village school. Soon another grand mansion, Middlesex House, comes into view. It was built in 1670 by John Fisher, who also owned a mill down by the brook. The number of large houses in close proximity is an indication of how much money was generated in this narrow valley when the clothing industry was at its height.

The building on the left with a sign bracket on its wall is the former Northend Inn, which closed in 2010. A little further along, on the side wall of the building on the corner of Seven Acres Lane, is a ghost sign for another pub, the Cooper's Arms, which closed in the 1950s.

Further along on the right, Northend Farm, probably mid-17th century, stands at right angles to the road. The gable adjoining the road looks different because this end of the building was restored and the gable end replaced in 1982. Then comes Northend House, early

Northend House, one of Batheaston's grander 17th-century properties, now subdivided, and known as Eagle Cottages

17th century and once owned by John Fisher, who also built Middlesex House. Just past it on the left is Eagle House (see pages 82-3).

As the pavement switches to the right-hand side of the road, its origins as a causeway can be clearly seen in the worn stone slabs. Just beyond Eagle Farmhouse, a pound, once used to confine stray livestock, can be seen on the right. Although you have now left the village behind, the succession of ancient buildings – some grand, some modest – continues intermittently as you head up St Catherine's Valley.

After passing the turning to Hollies Lane, at Myrtle Cottage the causeway switches back to the other side of the road. By Radford Farm, for the first time, there is an uninterrupted view across the valley. Then, by Oldhouse Farm, the causeway disappears before re-emerging from undergrowth and encroachments, establishing a pattern that continues as you head up the valley. A little further on, though, there is a particularly impressive raised section of causeway by Upper Northend Farm.

Heading north along St Catherine's Valley

When the lane forks, bear left uphill, following a sign for St Catherine (ST782693). As you pass Ranscombe Lane, look along it to see the sign for another long-lost pub, the Sandy Bank Inn, which closed in 1966. If the sight of all these lost pubs is making you thirsty, worse is soon to come, for, after passing Sandy Bank Farm, you reach the overgrown site of the legendary Mead Tea Gardens, which in their heyday attracted hundreds of people to this hidden valley on sunny summer afternoons.[1]

It is not just the Mead Tea Gardens that are no more. Virtually all trace of the causeway has now disappeared as you continue up the valley to St Catherine. After passing the old school, St Catherine's Court comes into view ahead. Arthur Mee, no stranger to hyperbole, went into overdrive when he came this way in 1940. 'It is incomparable,' he declared. 'We have seen nothing like it in our ten thousand villages more like the spirit of old England, tender, enduring, and altogether lovely. Flowing copper beeches, spreading chestnuts pink and white,

1 More on the gardens can be found at www.themeadteagardens.co.uk.

Sandy Bank Farm

St Catherine's Court and church

laburnums hanging with gold and lilacs with their royal stately purple, are everywhere about as St Catherine comes into view, and at St Catherine's gate we stand as if it were the gate of heaven. The gate of our English heaven it is, for there is nothing fairer in Somerset or in these islands.' Although the court is private, you can walk up the steps in front of it to visit the church, much of whose stained glass dates from the 15th century.

ST CATHERINE

'The situation is truly beautiful,' wrote the Rev John Collinson of St Catherine in 1791:

> The village stands on the declivity of a steep hill, called Holt Down, facing the east, and covered with wood, disposed in the most picturesque manner. A small rivulet winds through the vale beneath, which is composed of rich verdant meadows; and on its back rises another hill of about equal height, skirted with wood. The road hither from Batheaston, which is almost the only way to get to the village, is through dark lanes, overhung with trees and hedges, and in many places very steep and rocky. The precipitous height of Holt Down on the right, and the prospect to the left of a rich varied country, stretching to the Wiltshire hills, and the wildness and silent gloominess of the scenery around, render this solitary track, which is little visited by the traveller, pleasing and delightful; nor need we wonder that the monks of Bath should select the spot, for their retirement and devotion. They possessed this manor from very early times, and had here a grange, gardens, and a vineyard.

In 1086, the Prior of Bath Abbey leased the manor to Walter Hussey, and it is likely that he or one of his descendants built the chapel, which still contains Norman masonry. By 1258, the chapel was annexed to the church at Batheaston and the manor of St Catherine was managed directly by the Prior of Bath. A court roll of 1310 gives details of a barn where produce was stored before being despatched to the abbey, along with a fishpond and vineyards. The abbey also maintained a 'ewe flock' on Charmy Down. The grange or manor house, from where a steward or bailiff ran the estate, also seems to have been a popular country retreat for successive priors of Bath.

Around 1484, the manor was leased to Sir Thomas Fulford, Sheriff of Somerset and Dorset, but after his death in 1490 was taken back by Prior John Cantlow, who enlarged the church and may have started building the present court. In 1516, the manor was leased again, this time to William Harford, whose daughter Isabel married Thomas Llewellyn, the steward appointed by the prior. The lease was later transferred to Llewellyn, but in 1546, after the dissolution of Bath Abbey, Henry VIII granted the manor of St Catherine, along with that of Kelston, to Ethelreda Malte (see page 49). However, Llewellyn not only retained the lease, but handed it on to his eldest son, who held it until his death in 1582.

In 1591, John Blanchard of Marshfield leased St Catherine for an annual rent of £20 and two capons. He died the following year, but in 1594 his son bought the manor outright. It remained in the Blanchard family until 1747, by which time successive generations had transformed the court from a modest if substantial farmhouse into a fine manor house surrounded by terraced gardens. It was inherited by

Thomas Parry, a relation through marriage, and remained in his family until it was sold to Colonel Joseph Strutt in 1841. By then, it had fallen into disrepair and been divided into two properties, one of which was leased to a local farmer. Strutt set about restoring and remodelling the court, a process continued by his grandson Richard, who designed an extension, built a Doric-style orangery, added Jacobean-style plasterwork and panelling to several rooms, and created Italianate gardens.

St Catherine's Court in 1887 ...

... and around 1920 after the Italianate gardens had been built

In 1984, the actor Jane Seymour bought St Catherine's Court and carried out extensive refurbishments. It was used not only as a film set, but also as a recording studio by bands including The Cure, New Order and Radiohead, who recorded *OK Computer* here. Corporate events and weddings were also held, and these continued after the court was sold to an anonymous buyer in 2007. In December 2016, permission was granted for the building of a swimming pool and gym in the grounds to the west of the court.

This is where you have a choice between the shorter walk, which continues along St Catherine's Valley, and the longer walk, which heads north into Gloucestershire and the village of Marshfield.

● *For the shorter walk, carry on past St Catherine's Court and its 15th-century tithe barn. After 100m, opposite the entrance to The Loft, you will see a fishpond dating from when the prior of Bath owned*

St Catherine, with a magnificent stand of bamboo beside it. Continue as the lane rises past an ancient ivy-covered barn, with views across to Gloucestershire. Carry on past a turning on the right, and after 1100m you come

The Hermitage

to the Hermitage, which could almost be St Catherine's Court in miniature. Beyond it, the lane winds through woods to Cripp's Farm, where World War Two-style hangars stand alongside a building identified on old maps as Hermitage Cottage. Just past it on the left is a wayside well surrounded by a finely-wrought alcove. After passing a doggie daycare centre, you come to St Catherine's End House, opposite whose entrance you turn left up a footpath (ST761709).

Now skip to page 110, picking the directions up again at ●.

● *For the longer walk, carry on past the gates of St Catherine's Court for a few metres, before going through a metal kissing gate (KG) on the right, opposite the 15th-century tithe barn. Follow a faint track diagonally downhill, in the direction of the waymark. Go through another KG and carry straight on through a garden. After crossing a bridge over a spring, continue across another bridge over St Catherine's Brook and into Gloucestershire.*

The next mile or so may be a little tricky, not because of the conditions but because it is easy to mistake the route, which does not correspond with that shown on OS maps and includes a permissive rather than a public footpath. That said, the following directions should ensure you head in the right direction. Having crossed the bridge, bear right and cross a stile (which, unless it has been fixed, has a protruding nail to trip the unwary on the other side). *Carry on through*

*a field, following a faint and intermittent track as it climbs diago-
nally up to a telegraph pole, before continuing along the contours.
After crossing a stile by a metal gate, the track becomes a little*

*clearer. As you
come alongside a
hedge on the left,
look for a stile
with a permis-
sive path way-
mark* (ST783702),
*cross it and head
north through a
field (don't be
tempted to head
up to the gate on
the left). Cross a
stile at the end*
(ST785704), *carry*

The brook below St Catherine's Court, where you cross into Gloucestershire

*straight on through a meadow, cross another stile, turn right across
a final stile and turn left up a lane.*

*After 150m, turn left to follow a sign for Ashwicke. After 50m,
just before a gateway, turn right up steps, go through a KG and head
steeply uphill. Carry on past a KG in the fence on the right, and, after
a few metres, go through a KG ahead. Follow a faint track running
parallel with the fence below you, and head up to a KG at the far
end, where there is a superb view down the valley* (ST787713).

The pillar, Beek's Lane

*Turn left along a lane, following
it as it bears right past Ashwicke
Home Farm. After 100m, bear left
through a seven-bar gate, where a
waymark post points along Dukwick
Lane. For the first 300m, you follow
a rough track alongside a hedge, but
at the end of the field, you continue
along a fully-fledged green lane.
When you come to a tarmaced lane,
bear right to carry on along it.*

*After 120m, bear left along a
bridleway signposted to Marshfield*
(ST777718). *After 250m, carry
straight on across another track,
and, after another 1000m, when
you come to Beek's Lane*, you will

see an 18th-century pillar on the left. The inscription on it, now very worn, reads, 'TO BEEKS HOUSE / Turn on the right track / Over the down / Drivers of carriages / are desired to / keep the road made / Over the down'. Beek's House was a large mansion, demolished sometime after 1785, which stood a mile to the south near a mill on St Catherine's Brook.

Turn right along Beek's Lane for 1000m, turning left at the end and then right along Sheepfair Lane. After 200m, turn right along Weir Lane. The weed-choked pond you pass on the left was a carriage wash. The buildings behind it formed part of Marshfield Brewery, which closed in the 1880s, apparently after the bursting of a huge vat of beer drove the owners into bankruptcy. The fascinating range of old buildings off to the right included one of Marshfield's many malthouses.

The weed-choked carriage wash at Marshfield

Old buildings on Weir Lane

At the top, turn right by the old school and right again into the Market Place. The building on your left with a large sign bracket was the Codrington Arms, also known as the King's Arms, which closed in 1931. *After passing the old vicarage on the right, follow the lane as it curves left out of the Market Place. After 100m, bear left when the lane forks, and after a few metres double back along a path leading through the churchyard. Carry on along Church Lane, passing the entrance to the manor on your right. Once back in the Market Place, turn right to head along a narrow street.* After 50m, look to your right across a yard to see a 16th-century dovecote in the grounds of the manor.

At the end, turn left past the Lord Nelson Inn 🍺 and follow the road as it curves right along the High Street. Until the bypass opened in 1967 this was the main road from London to Bristol, and in the 18th century there were several inns to cater for the coaching trade. The two most important were the Crown, open by 1650 but currently closed, and the Catherine Wheel 🍺, built as a private

house around 1690 and converted to an inn around 50 years later. The Lord Nelson came along somewhat later, probably opening soon after Nelson's victory and death at Trafalgar.

Marshfield High Street is a delight, lined with a superb array of buildings

The manorial dovecote

Marshfield in the late 19th-century

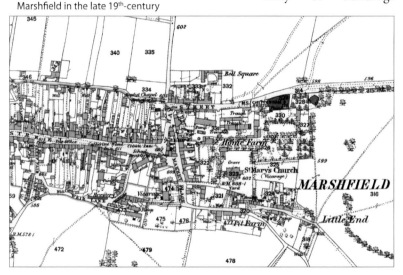

– from cottages to mansions, and with a good scattering of shops, sheds, stables, alleys and malthouses – dating from the 16th to the 19th centuries. Largely unspoilt and in many cases painstakingly restored, it is a street to take your time over. And, although far less famous than nearby Lacock and Castle Combe, it is no less rewarding – a hidden gem well worth seeking out and savouring. There is, however, little of interest north of the High Street, and, apart from a few buildings, most of which you saw earlier, little to the south. It is very much a one-street village – but what a glorious street.[1]

1 A good introduction to Marshfield's history can be found in Leech, *Small Medieval Towns in Avon*; see also www.marshfieldparish.org.uk/wp/marshfield-history/intro.htm.

MARSHFIELD

MARSHFIELD was established as a 'new town' around 1265, when it was granted a charter to hold a market. When a tax assessment was made in 1334, it was the fourth richest town in Gloucestershire, after Bristol, Gloucester and Cirencester. In medieval times, its prosperity came from the wool trade, but by the beginning of the 18th century, malt, made from barley grown in fields around the town, was the most important industry, with around 80 malthouses supplying breweries in Bath and Bristol. In 1779, however, Samuel Rudder, in his *History of Gloucestershire*, wrote that 'the business of making malt to supply the cities of Bath and Bristol ... has been for some time declining'.

The decline continued; by 1870 there were only eight malthouses left, and by 1891 the number had dropped to three. By 1901, Marshfield's population stood at 1,223, slightly less than it had been a century earlier. History, and industrialisation, had passed Marshfield by, and the town that was once one of the most prosperous in the county had dwindled to little more than a village.

Marshfield in 1887

Decline, however, meant that little was altered, little was pulled down, and the town's original layout was preserved almost intact. This consisted of burgage plots laid out on either side of the High Street, many extending back over 100m, with lanes running behind them. Malthouses were established on a large number of these plots and survive today as long outhouses behind many of the buildings along the High Street.

The High Street ends abruptly, after 300m, by the 17th-century Crispe Almshouses. Continue on for another 150m, before turning left beside an old tollhouse along Green Lane (ST772737), *which soon degenerates to a rough track winding downhill. At the bottom, follow it as it bears right and, after another 120m, cross a stile on the right to head down St Catherine's Valley* (ST772732).

Green Lane

The headwaters of St Catherine's Valley

After going through a KG, head through a tunnel of trees beside the brook, carry on and go through another KG. When you see several paths ahead, take the most trodden one on the left. When you come to where another valley branches off uphill to the right, follow a path curving left between trees to carry on down St Catherine's Valley (ST760726). *Although the path is less distinct here – seemingly disappearing altogether at times – if you stick roughly to the contour line, after 400m you should see a fence a little way below you on the left.*

Go through a KG at the end and head left downhill, bearing to the left of the overgrown hedge ahead and crossing a slab bridge across the brook at the bottom (ST759721). *Follow the path as it bears right uphill and cross a stile. Do not be tempted to turn left alongside the fence, but head uphill for a few metres before turning left and following a rough path as it curves along the contour line.*

After crossing a stile, carry on alongside a hedge on the left, cross another stile and, when you come to a lane, turn left (ST760712). *Follow the lane as it curves downhill past a 17th-century farmhouse and carry on, with Monkswood Reservoir above you on the right.* As you cross a stream with a pumping station beside it, you cross the county boundary back into Somerset. It was near here, during the construction of the reservoir, that 38 pieces of bronze age metal-work, known as the Monkswood Hoard, were discovered. *After the lane swings left, it passes Paper Mill Cottage* – its name recalling a long-forgotten industry in this hidden valley –

Looking over St Catherine's Valley

before climbing steeply. Opposite the imposing gateway of St Catherine's End House, bear right up a footpath (ST761709).

● *Here the shorter walk along St Catherine's Valley links up with the longer walk.*

Head up through a gate, carry on up steps and go through a KG. Continue uphill with a high hedge on your left. Go through a KG and follow a path up through woodland – which after heavy rain is likely to be running with multifarious springs. *After going through another KG, follow a track as it bears steeply up to the right. When you come to a farm track, bear left up it and follow it as it curves right to a metal gate.* Before going through the gate, turn to look back across the valley where Beek's Farm, with an old barn beside it, can be seen on the opposite hillside.

Go through the gate and follow a waymark towards another KG. To your right can be seen ruinous structures connected with the airfield built here in 1940. *Once through the KG, carry on across the plateau, watching out for electric fences and heading to the left of the right-hand clump of trees ahead.* This track follows the course of one of the airfield's three runways. Had you come this way before the airfield was built, you would have found a landscape little changed for millennia, with a group of five barrows to your left and the remains of Romano-British field systems beyond. All were flattened to build the airfield, which has in turn reverted to nature, albeit nature of a bleak and vestigial kind. Beyond the distant perimeter of this dreary plateau all that can be seen of the hills that ring the city are the heights of Lansdown, enlivened by the distinctive profile of Beckford's Tower. At 236m, Lansdown is the only place around Bath that looks down on Charmy Down's 212m. In the distance, though, the caterpillar of trees on Freezing Hill can once again be seen. Charmy Down feels not only remote and cut off from the outside world, but also somehow drained of any sense of continuity or link with the past, the legacy of the vital role it played in Britain's war effort. And, although grass now covers the runways of RAF Charmy Down, it still feels like a brownfield site.

After passing the trees, go through a metal gate and carry straight on. On the far side of the airfield, where you will see some pillboxes to your left, turn right alongside a fence and follow a gravel track as it swings left through a gate. When you come to another gate, squeeze past it and follow the lane ahead downhill (ST760694). *After 800m, you pass Uplands Farm. Carry on for another 250m, before going through a KG on the left. Follow a waymark sign across the field and turn right alongside the hedge. Go through a KG and carry straight on between hedges. After going through another KG* (ST766681), *carry on uphill through ground disturbed by quarrying. When you see a mizmaze* (see pages 90 & 92) *to your right, turn past it and head south along a rough path past rocky outcrops, with the ramparts of Little Solsbury above.*

After 300m, with a trig point up to your left, head down to a bench below you. Bear right when you reach it and follow a rough and muddy track through humps and bumps gradually downhill. The track is unclear in places, but carry on in the same direction until you find it broadening and curving more steeply downhill to a KG by a seven-bar gate. Go through the KG and bear left alongside the hedgerow. After going through another KG at the end of the field, turn right along a lane for 35m and then left along a footpath (ST765675). *When you come to another lane, continue along a footpath a few metres over to the left. Carry straight on past the backs of buildings to emerge on Bailbrook Lane. Here you have a choice.*

To return to Batheaston, from where you can catch a bus back to Bath, turn left for a few metres before turning right down a footpath. Carry on down steps and along a road. At a T junction turn right downhill, and, when you come to the main road, cross and turn left for 150m to a bus stop.

To walk back to Bath, turn right along Bailbrook Lane. After 300m, continue across Gloucester Road and head down Ferndale Road. At the T junction at the bottom, turn left, continue past the Bladud's Head and carry on through Larkhall, before joining the London Road to head back to the city centre.

Charmy Down: A Lost Landscape

Most Bathonians will have heard of Charmy Down, possibly because of the Park & Ride car park the council, after prolonged deliberation, decided not to build there, or possibly because of the RAF station established there in the Second World War. Unless they are keen walkers, however, or enjoy visiting old airfields, it is likely to be just a name. Of all the high hills around Bath, Charmy Down is the least visited and the least known.

It has a fascinating history, though. In the bronze age, seven round barrows were raised here. Five of them were in a group, forming a prominent feature. In 1822, the Rev John Skinner of Camerton, a prodigious amateur antiquarian and archaeologist, surveyed and excavated them, only to discover that they had already been plundered by treasure seekers. In the 1840s, James Tunstall described the down as being

> covered with British earthworks and intrenchments, of which I have in vain sought for an account. In the field immediately behind the house is a Druid's temple, similar to Stanton Drew. One stone still stands; although the others are half hidden by the turf, the circle may still be traced. In 'Tumpy Field', the plough has passed through several long ridges of ancient stone heaps, and in it are four barrows, the largest of which I measured, and found it to be 100 yards in circumference and 20 feet high; these will soon be obliterated by the plough.

Much of the down seems to have been divided up into small fields bounded by earth banks. Although these probably predated the arrival of the Romans, they may have continued in use into the Roman period. Most of this field system was destroyed by ploughing before a survey of the down was carried out, but four small groups of fields survived into the 20th century.

In the middle ages, Charmy Down formed part of the Manor of St Catherine (or Katherine as it was sometimes known) and was owned by the Prior of Bath Abbey, who grazed sheep here. It remained part of the Manor of St Catherine after the Reformation, and in 1749, shortly after Thomas Parry inherited the manor, he advertised 'Charmy Down, about 200 acres; and also a farm adjoining containing about 260 acres of arable and pasture land' to let.

In the following year, Charmy Down was bought outright by the governors of Bath's Mineral Water Hospital, who leased it to a tenant.

Opposite: Modern ruins on Charmy Down

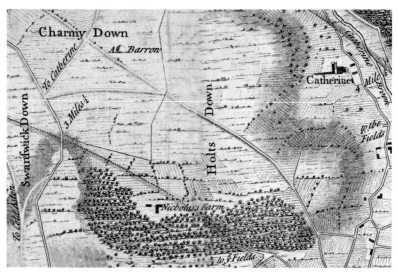

Charmy Down on Thorpe's map of 1742

In 1870, the governors of the hospital leased part of the down to Bath Corporation so that reservoirs could be built to supply water to the city, and in 1920 they sold the entire down to the corporation.

All the changes that had taken place since people first set foot on Charmy Down, however, paled into insignificance compared with what happened next. As early as the 1920s, there had been calls for Bath to have an aerodrome. Two impromptu airfields were actually established – near the racecourse on Lansdown, and at Norwoods Farm on Claverton Down (which now lies under the university's sports training village). Lansdown was always the preferred location for a permanent aerodrome, but, as this would have taken a sizeable chunk of land from the golf club, it naturally aroused a good deal of vociferous – and influential – opposition.

Then, in 1936, the air ministry contacted the council 'on the subject of possible aerodrome sites in the neighbourhood of Bath', expressing the view that Lansdown would be the best site and Charmy Down the second best. As much of Bath's water supply now came from Charmy Down's springs, the council asked for the view of their waterworks committee, who replied that, 'in view of the paramount importance of ensuring the purity of the water supply, they could not recommend the city council to consent to any portion of the catchment area at Charmy Down being utilised for the purpose of an aerodrome'.

By now, the council had ruled out Claverton as a possible site for an aerodrome and turned down an application for one on Lansdown 'to the relief of the Races Committee, the Golf Club, and residents in the vicinity'. If they hoped the matter would go away, the air ministry soon put them right, and in October 1937 applied to the waterworks committee to use part of Charmy Down as a 'practice forced landing ground'. The committee once again regretted that they were 'unable to accede to the application'. When the air ministry asked them to reconsider, they instructed the town clerk to reply that they were 'unable to depart from their previous decision'. A year later, the air ministry contacted the council again 'with regard to the possibility of land at Charmy Down being used for Air Force purposes'. Again, the council replied that they were 'unable to allow its use for any purpose which might endanger the purity of the water supply to the city'.

At which stage, with war looming, the matter was taken out of the council's hands, and the next we hear of Charmy Down is of a hurried archaeological investigation being carried out prior to an airfield being built. RAF Charmy Down opened late in 1940, with grass landing strips, which were replaced with concrete runways the following year. In 1943, an exercise took place, in which the Bath Home Guard was entrusted to defend the airfield against an attack from the Bristol Home Guard. Apparently, 'local rivalry added a spice to the occasion and fists and arms were used in a most unorthodox fashion', and the exercise was brought to a hasty conclusion. The airfield was later used by the US Air Force, before being returned to the RAF at the end of the war.

For a time, it seemed that it might become a civil airport. In July 1945, the newly-formed West of England Civil Air Transport Committee decided that the airfield at Filton, home to the Bristol

Charmy Down today

Aeroplane Company, should become 'a great continental airport serving the West of England', and that Charmy Down 'should serve as a landing strip "feeding" the West airport'.

The *Bath Chronicle* was keen on the idea, as it would mean that 'people from the continent would be able to avail themselves of the Bath waters in a matter of hours'. This, however, was the last that was heard of the scheme, and on 7 June 1946, the *Chronicle* revealed that 'the Charmy Down RAF Station, which went off the active list at Christmas, is now manned by only 30 maintenance men. What is to be its future no one apparently knows, least of all the staff there. It is like some outpost of Empire, with rare callers.'

Four months later, uncertainty over the camp's future was resolved when a Mr Jones, who had been stationed there during the war, returned with his wife and two small children, and moved into one of the empty huts. 'Squatters have moved into the RAF Camp at Charmy Down,' announced the *Chronicle*, adding that the hut Mr Jones had chosen 'is one of the few that possess flush-type lavatories, bath and wash-basins. It is built of brick and asbestos, is in excellent condition, and has four rooms in addition to the kitchen, bathroom and lavatory. There is running water, but, as yet, no electricity.'

Other families soon followed, most of them having no connection with the airfield. They simply had nowhere else to go. A council spokesman was unsympathetic. 'We do not want squatters there,' he declared, 'and we are taking every precaution in view of the danger of contaminating water supplies.' Given the desperate post-war housing situation, however, when the Ministry of Health offered the council a temporary lease of the domestic accommodation at Charmy Down two months later, they agreed to take it on.

By the end of 1946, there were around 40 families at Charmy Down, paying five shillings a week rent. The following year, a shop, a clinic and a 'fish and chip saloon' had opened. Buses between Bath and Marshfield were diverted to call at the airfield, and within a couple of years a church and a junior school for 120 children had been provided. The rows of huts were given names – Cedar Grove and Ash Grove. An application by the landlord of the Bladud Arms in Swainswick to open an off licence at the camp was, however, refused.

Despite the residents paying rent to the council, they continued to be referred to as squatters, which not surprisingly they took exception to. On 3 January 1948, Mr E Lawson of 29 Ash Grove, Charmy Down, who had converted part of his hut to a general store, wrote to the *Chronicle* insisting that 'we are bona fide tenants of Bathavon RDC, and as such resent the term of "squatter" being used to describe us. There is a vast difference,' he continued, 'between a squatter and a person who

Pillboxes at the southern end of Charmy Down

pays rent, and I believe that out of about 130 families now residing here, only four were originally squatters.'

Although the council may have been receiving rent from the residents of Charmy Down, they were reluctant to upgrade the facilities of what were essentially Nissen huts, put up quickly and cheaply and with no intention for them to be occupied on anything other than a temporary basis. A month after Mr Lawson wrote to the *Chronicle*, the chairman of the local magistrates complained that 'this bench is continually having the circumstances of the Charmy Down Camp brought to our notice, and the magistrates feel that the Bathavon Rural District Council and the Ministry of Health should provide much better amenities at the huts if they are going to allow people to continue to live there.'

The council could have decided to instigate a programme of upgrading or replacing the huts with permanent houses, the nucleus of an estate that could eventually have covered more of the disused airfield. Instead, the community was dispersed, the buildings demolished and the runways grassed over. Today, although the ruins of a few buildings – most notably the former control tower – survive, the view across this hilltop plateau is a desolate one. Charmy Down, although returned to agricultural use, exists in an eerie limbo, not quite a brownfield site, still less the breezy stretch of downland it once was. Faced with an ever-worsening housing shortage, in an area where suitable development land is at a premium, could the time be ripe for re-establishing a community on the hilltop where people first settled four millennia ago?

The Avon Valley: Walk 9
Trains & Boats & Planes

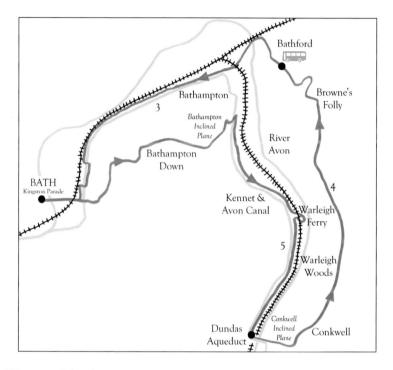

Distance: 12 miles;
   a shorter option is available by catching a bus (3) from Bathford to
   Bath at the end of the walk

Terrain: Some rough paths, steps, steep slopes and possible muddy
   sections

Pubs and cafés:
   Angelfish Café, Brassknocker Basin (500m south of Dundas
   Aqueduct) (01225 723483)

Map: OS Explorer 155 or AA Walker's Map 25

Opposite: Dundas Aqueduct

This walk follows the Avon valley upstream to Dundas, following the towpath of the Kennet & Avon Canal, which runs alongside the railway. That accounts for the boats and trains – the planes come in the form of two gravity-operated tramways, otherwise known as inclined planes, down which stone travelled to canalside wharves. Quarries which produced the stone are also visited, so there is much for anyone interested in industrial archaeology or transport history to enjoy. This is, though, very much a walk for everyone, with the glorious scenery of the Avon valley contrasting with the twisting paths and rocky outcrops of the hills above.

From Kingston Parade, head east along York Street. Turn right at the end and bear left by the Huntsman pub along North Parade. Cross at the lights, carry on along North Parade and cross at the lights at the end of North Parade Road. Bear left for a few metres before turning through an archway under the railway bridge. Follow a path up steps to the canal and turn right along the towpath. After 75m, turn left across a footbridge and continue up a path. After crossing a road, carry on in the same direction, passing a road on the left, but, after another 120m, turn left along a path to emerge on Bathwick Hill. Cross and head along Cleveland Walk for 600m.

At the end, turn right up North Road, and after 50m cross and go through a gate onto National Trust land. Walk up a broad sunken track down which Bath stone was once carried. After 250m, when you see a bench on the left, bear right through a kissing gate (KG) and bear left alongside a fence (ST766652). *Do not follow a Skyline waymark pointing right, but carry straight on along a track winding through the woods. After crossing a path with a waymark post, you reach a clearing, where a broad swathe of trees has been cleared to accommodate overhead cables, affording the dubious privilege of a panoramic view of the Batheaston bypass.*

As you plunge back into the woods, the track grows ever rougher. After passing a path branching left, go through a KG and head uphill to emerge on Bathampton Down. Bear left uphill, and after 400m, as you approach the woods, bear right up towards a bench. After passing it, carry on towards a post at the corner of a barbed-wire fence where a waymark points to a KG into the woods (ST775655).

After going through the KG, carry on for 250m before crossing a metal stile which leads onto a path heading steeply downhill. This follows the course of an inclined plane which carried stone down to a wharf on the canal. Our route follows the plane downhill, but, if you first want to visit the quarry where the stone came from, go through a gap in the fence a little way along to the right and follow a path through flower-rich grassland to emerge in a hidden amphitheatre, its man-made cliffs pierced by the entrances to underground workings.

After following the course of the plane downhill for 400m, the footpath diverges away from it to the left. A little further on, when a track curves in from the right, look along it to see a bridge which carried the plane over the old road from Claverton to Bathampton (ST780657).

Above: Stone sleepers on the Bathampton Plane

Left: The plane on the first Ordnance Survey map, which predated the construction of the Warminster Road

Below: The bridge which carried the plane over the old road from Claverton to Bathampton

THE BATHAMPTON PLANE

The first reference to the inclined plane at Bathampton comes in an advertisement in the *Bath Chronicle* on 18 June 1808:

> ANY Person or Persons willing to CONTRACT for forming, making, and compleating an INCLINED PLANE ROAD from Bath-Hampton Quarries to the Kennet and Avon Canal, a distance of about 800 yards, are desired to send their proposals (sealed up) to Mr Bennett, engineer, St James's Parade, Bath – Plans, sections, and specifications may be seen at Mr Bennett's office.

William Bennett (or Bennet) had been appointed engineer to the Somersetshire Coal Canal in 1795. Around 1807, when the company found itself in financial difficulties after he seriously underestimated the cost of building locks at Combe Hay, he was dismissed. His experience of building inclined planes for the canal company, however, led him to conclude that building one here, as an alternative to the steep rutted tracks in use up till then, would be just the thing.

The inclined plane opened around 1810, and, according to the Rev John Skinner, was built 'nearly on the line of a British road' – in other words, an ancient trackway. It was 'self-acting', with descending wagons, loaded with stone, hauling up empty ones which had been unloaded at the wharf. The two tracks on which the wagons ran had a gauge of three feet four inches, and the rails were of cast iron. The wagons were attached to a rope wound round a drum at the top of the plane, which ran over friction rollers laid between the rails. The wagons, which could carry up to 70 cwt (3556 kg) of stone, consisted of a wooden platform surrounded by an iron railing.

In 1819, when that indefatigable traveller, Pierce Egan, visited this 'iron rail-way' descending 'from an immense steep height', he wrote that

> it is curious to observe the iron carriages sent up and down without horses; and by the aid of machinery the vehicles change their positions midway, the full one running down to the barge in the canal, and the empty one making its way to the top again to receive its load.

The plane had a relatively short life. Although an arch was constructed in the early 1830s to carry it over the newly-built Warminster Road, it seems to have been abandoned soon afterwards, and by the mid-1840s, James Tunstall could write that 'the railroad is destroyed and covered with turf', and the canal wharf is 'now disused'.

Many of the stone sleepers on which rails rested survive, but, as you head down the plane today, with the ground contorted by over a century and a half of subsidence, erosion and tree-root encroachment, it is difficult to imagine what a robust and well-constructed piece of engineering this would once have been.[1]

1 See Bodman, *Inclined Planes*; Pollard, 'Bath Stone Quarry Railways'

Beyond this, the footpath carries on to join the main road, whose construction was the reason for the footpath's diversion. The Warminster Road was authorised by act of parliament in 1833 and completed a couple of years later. As it cut through the plane, which was still in use, a bridge had to be built to carry the plane across it. Known as the Dry Arch, this bridge was a well-known local landmark, and long survived the abandonment of the plane shortly afterwards. In 1958, though, it finally fell victim to road improvements.

The Dry Arch over the Warminster Road in the early 20th-century

A wintry view from the 1980s of the plane below the Dry Arch, running down to Hampton Quarry Wharf

This means that, ***to carry on down the plane, you need to make a detour, crossing the road, and turning right along the pavement. After 150m, when the pavement ends, a left turn, following a high-hedged footpath through a gate, leads back to the plane. At the bottom is Hampton Quarry Wharf,*** which still looks much as it did when stone was transhipped from wagons to boats for the next stage of its journey.

After crossing the swing bridge (you may have to wait if a boat is passing), turn right along the towpath, keeping a watch out for cyclists. From here, there is an excellent view of Browne's Folly, on the edge of Farleigh Down, with the Avon flowing

placidly below and trains rattling past.

The walk along the canal is enlivened by a succession of boats, each an expression of artistry and personality, decorated in styles ranging from traditional to new age – and beyond – often with more than a dash of whimsy. In an age when bland conformity is ever more the rule, it is good to see such individuality and creativity thriving.

After about 500m, the canal swings away from the river and the railway, before swinging back again and passing under Bridge 181. Across the valley the towers and turrets of Warleigh Manor can be seen rising above the trees. Built around 1815 for Henry Skrine, the manor remained in the Skrine family until 1956, after which it was used as a school. It has now been converted back to residential use.

Just before you come to the next bridge, there is a short diversion. Turn left down the lane beside the canal and cross the railway at the bottom. After crossing the line, you will see what looks like a mill on the left. It is in fact a pumping station, built on the site of a mill by John Rennie, the canal engineer. Unlike

The canal near Claverton

Claverton Pumping Station

most pumping stations, it was powered not by coal but by water. When the sluices were opened, water from the river flowed along the leat and turned a large waterwheel. This drove beam engines which pumped the water up to the canal, a solution both ingenious and elegant, and an early example of green technology. The pumping station ceased operation in 1952, but 15 years later restoration got under way, and it starting pumping water again in 1975. Today it only operates occasionally, however, as the water level is maintained by two electric pumps installed upstream by British Waterways in 1981. In 2017, after a four-year restoration project, it was once again returned to working order, and can be visited on open days throughout the summer (visit www.claverton.org for information). The cottage on the other side of the railway line, meanwhile, predates just about everything else in this busy scene; built in the 17th century – possibly earlier – it was probably associated with the corn mill that once stood here.

Having crossed the bridge over the leat, cross a stile into the meadow. A road, which may have dated from Roman times, once ran here. Its course can be seen on the 19th-century map below, and,

Warleigh Weir

A late 19th-century OS map showing Claverton Pumping Station, somewhat unaccountably, as a disused mill, along with Warleigh Weir and Ferry, and the course of the road leading to the ford across the river

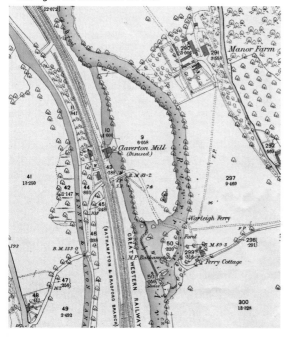

if you turn right, its outline starts to appear as a sunken way, growing ever deeper as it nears the river. At the river's brink, with the water tumbling over the weir, it seems impossible that there was once a ford here, a ford, moreover, that veered left to skirt round a small island before making landfall on the far bank some 100m away. This sunken way also formed part of a ditch dug by Parliamentary forces in the Civil War to protect a temporary bridge which guarded the southern approaches to the city of Bath. On 3 July 1642, however, Royalist forces routed Parliamentary soldiers stationed on the east side of the valley and laid siege to the bridgehead, which they took after fierce fighting. With the river crossing now in control of the Royalists, Parliamentary forces encamped on the west side of the valley withdrew to Bath, leaving the Royalists to continue their advance north. Two days later, the opposing armies met at the Battle of Lansdown.[1]

If you turn left alongside the river, you will come to a rough flight of steps, with a similar flight of steps on the opposite bank. This was the site of Warleigh Ferry, which was operated using a cable stretched across the river, and worked by a ferryman who lived in a cottage on the far bank. From 1882 to 1925, the ferryman was Charles Jones, a Crimean veteran who was described by the *Bath Chronicle* as 'an old gentleman well known to up-river picnic parties, many of which, in the summertime, stop to take tea at his cottage'. He was succeeded by William Trebble, another naval veteran, who operated the ferry until the late 1940s, when John Byrne took over. The ferry remained popular, especially during the summer, when up to 200 a people a day made the crossing, many of them walkers who took tea in the gardens of the ferryman's cottage.

At such times, Warleigh Ferry was a delightful spot, but when the river was in flood it was a different story. On several occasions the boat was swept away. Usually, it became entangled in a fallen tree or some other obstacle a few hundred yards downstream, but once it almost reached Bath and had to be towed back by Sea Scouts when the waters subsided. In 1951, however, it was so badly damaged by floodwaters that a new boat, called somewhat whimsically the Queen Mary, was brought into service. By now, the fare for the crossing, which in Charles Jones's day was a halfpenny, had risen to twopence.

In 1956, the ferry was taken over by George Cornell. Four years later, in 1960, he handed over to John Guilfoyle, who had only been there a few months when the area was hit by the worst floods for years. Despite efforts to keep the cable across the river clear of debris, such was the weight of the material forced against it that it eventually snapped, spelling the end of the ferry forever. Almost 60 years later, two broken-down flights of steps hidden away on a tree-shaded stretch of the River Avon are the only reminder of the lost ferry of Warleigh.

After that interlude, it is time to **head back to the canal and carry on along the towpath.** For a time, you can continue to enjoy this glorious valley in peace, disturbed only by the occasional rattle of passing trains, until the canal curves back towards the road by Millbrook swing bridge. After another 500m, a bridge comes into

---

1 For an account of the skirmish, see Wroughton, *The Battle of Lansdown: An Explorer's Guide*

view ahead, heralding the approach to Dundas Basin, where boats laden with coal from the Somerset coalfield joined the Kennet & Avon. As you pass the bridge (staying on the left bank), the lock which controlled access to the Somersetshire Coal Canal can be seen ahead. The Coal Canal was abandoned in the early twentieth century, and only the first 500m is navigable today, having been restored to create a private marina. Unfortunately, the stone bridge which carried the towpath over the lock entrance was demolished after the canal closed and the lock was filled in, but the survival of a 19th-century crane and warehouse still give some sense of what Dundas Basin would have been like in its industrial heyday.[1]

In this engraving by JC Nattes, showing Dundas Aqueduct shortly after it opened in 1804, the inclined plane built to carry stone down from the quarry at Conkwell can be seen in the background

If you are need of refreshment at this point, the Angelfish café can be found at the far end of the marina, access to which is along the path to the left of the marina entrance. Getting there entails crossing the canal, as well as making a lengthy detour, but, as the next part of the walk includes a stiff climb, you may well consider it worthwhile.

1 More on the Coal Canal can be found on pages 135-6 and in walks 10 to 12.

***Continue along the
left bank of the canal
as it makes a 90-degree
turn to stride across the
valley on a magnificent
aqueduct.*** The railway,
which came later than
the canal – and took
most of its trade away –
also tunnels beneath the
aqueduct. On a fine day,
there can be few more
inspiring spots than this
– it even has its own
soundtrack, an evocative
melody called *Dundas*
written by composer
and English concertina
player Rob Harbron
when he was moored up
on a narrowboat here.[1]

Dundas Aqueduct in the late 19ᵗʰ-century

Looking north from the aqueduct

As you cross the
aqueduct, you pass the
boathouses of Monkton
Combe School. Beyond
them, you will see an embankment curving across the field towards the
river. This is thought to have carried a tramway, the continuation of
an inclined plane which brought stone down from a quarry to build
the aqueduct. ***On the far side of the aqueduct, head to the left of
a large hut, and, when the path forks, bear left to cross a stile. As
you head uphill, you are following the course of that inclined plane.***
Like the Bathampton plane, this was a double-track, self-acting, rope-
worked incline, with descending wagons, loaded with stone, hauling up
empty ones. It was built by the canal company in 1800 to supply stone
for aqueducts, bridges, locks and other structures. However, the stone
was of indifferent quality and the company soon turned elsewhere for
its supplies. The sleepers, unlike those on the Bathampton Plane, were
wooden and were lifted and sold when the plane closed in 1812.

The course of the tramway may not be too apparent at first, but, ***after
crossing another stile, you enter woodland and soon find yourself
heading up through a cutting. When the fence on the right ends at***

1 You can find it at robertharbron.com/?p=152.

the top of the plane (ST790623), *turn left along a crosspath and carry on into the hamlet of Conkwell.* This was once something of a Mecca for daytrippers from Bath. In the late 19th century, REM Peach described it as 'especially worthy of a visit. Placed, like Petra

The Conkwell Inclined Plane

of old, in a cleft of the rocks, it exhibits, perhaps, greater marks of antiquity than almost any other cluster of houses in the kingdom. No admirer of sylvan scenery should visit Bath and leave this old world village unseen.' Tea gardens offered refreshment to thirsty ramblers, and on sunny summer weekends this remote spot would have been crowded with those who had escaped from the city for a few hours.

After turning right uphill, turn left along the road at the top for 350m, before turning left along a lane signposted to Warleigh (ST795628). This quiet byway, winding through Warleigh Woods, is a delight, and it is likely that your walk will only be interrupted by the occasional car. *After 650m, you will see a stile by a metal gate on the right. Carry on past it, but, 150m further on, when the lane bears left downhill, carry straight on along a rough and rocky waymarked footpath into the woods* (ST798636).

After passing a wooden bench (which, before trees grew up to obscure it, commanded a splendid view over the valley), *the track forks. Take the main fork to the right, and, with the track growing ever rougher, when you see a stone wall on your right, look for another fork, and follow a 'Bradford on Avon Walking Wheel' waymark down a stepped path* – but take your time. Some of the steps are well camouflaged to trip the unwary, and the path is steep.

When you come to another wall, bear right uphill under a bridge known – like that which carried the plane over the road at Bathampton – as the Dry Arch. This arch was built in 1795 to carry the road from Bathford to Bradford on Avon over a track which, in its unswerving descent, may look like another plane, but is in fact an old road down to the ferry at Warleigh. It was once known as the Roman Road, and may indeed date back to Roman times.

After going through the arch, turn left alongside a wall, and, when you come to a busy road, carry on along the verge. Extreme care needs to be exercised here – especially if you have children or

BROWNE'S FOLLY

Browne's Folly has long been an enigma. Wade Browne, who commissioned it, was born in Leeds in 1796 and settled at Monkton Farleigh Manor around 1836. He became High Sheriff of Wiltshire, was a noted benefactor, and died in 1851. On 14 September 1848, the *Bath Chronicle* reported that 'a lofty tower has recently been erected by Wade Brown [sic], Esq, on Farleigh Down, the summit of which commands one of the most extensive and magnificent prospects in our neighbourhood. The building has added a decidedly picturesque feature to the scenery of our vicinity. Seen from some positions, it has a very fine effect.' No indication, though, of why it was built.

Not until 1934, when urgent repairs to the tower were carried out, funded by a bequest from one of Wade Browne's daughters, did the *Chronicle* become curious as to the reason for its construction, and published a request for information. There were numerous replies. Someone suggested it had been built for 'government surveying purposes', another that it 'replaced a semaphore which had been erected by the government surveyors in the time of the Welsh riots'. Then again, according to 'local tradition', it was built 'to assist in the relief of unemployment during the period of economic depression which followed the close of the Napoleonic Wars' – even though the Battle of Waterloo had been fought 33 years earlier.[1] More recently, it has been suggested that, as the quarries on Wade Browne's estate were going through a lean period, he built the tower to advertise his stone as well as to provide work for the quarrymen.[2]

As for it being a semaphore tower, this can be discounted. The country's most important line of semaphore stations, linking

1 *Bath Chronicle*, 13 October 1934; 14 April 1934.
2 See www.avonwildlifetrust.org.uk/reserves/brownes-folly.

the Admiralty in London with Portsmouth, was completed in 1822 but decommissioned in 1847 when the development of the electric telegraph rendered it obsolete. It is hardly likely that a new semaphore tower would have been built a year later. Given Wade Browne's record as a benefactor, however, and the harsh economic climate of 'the hungry forties', the likelihood is that it was built to provide work for local people – as well as giving Wade Browne the satisfaction of leaving a permanent – and undeniably pleasing – mark on the landscape.

This is borne out by a report in the *Bath Chronicle* on 14 June 1888 of a sale of work at Monkton Farleigh Manor. It was organised by Lady Hobhouse, whose husband had bought the manor in 1873, and one of the items on sale was 'a brief but succinct history of the manor house from the pen ... of its present owner'. According to this,

> the house and grounds were greatly altered and improved during Mr Wade Browne's occupation. This gentleman was a real benefactor to the parish. He not only furnished a reservoir of water for general use but found work for the parishioners when it was scarce in building the tower on Farleigh Down (now so conspicuous and familiar an object in the landscape) and in improving the roads. He was likewise a generous donor to the village school.

Which seems as close as we are likely to get to a definitive answer as to why it was built. As for who designed it, however, and what, if any, celebrations were held to mark its completion, that must remain, for the moment at least, a mystery.

The Dry Arch built in 1795 to carry the Bath to Bradford on Avon road over a track once known as the Roman Road

dogs with you – for, even though you do not walk in the road, the verge is narrow. Yet this is a well-walked footpath, with no feasible alternative available. Widening the verge even a little would make it safer and more user-friendly.

After 125m, bear right following a broken footpath sign past a stile into woods (ST796645). As the track curves away from the road and climbs, with the land shelving ever more steeply away on the left, look up to see where quarries and caves have been hollowed out of the hillside. *When the track eventually levels out beside a wall, carry on along it, ignoring footpaths heading down to the left.* The track leads into Browne's Folly Nature Reserve, where you may notice some blue posts, erected by the Bath Geological Society to identify rocks and fossils.[1]

When you reach Browne's Folly (ST794660)*, turn left through a KG to follow a stepped path curving steeply downhill. At the bottom, two paths head right across grassland. Take the upper one along a ridge* with a panoramic view over the Avon valley and to the caterpillar of trees on Freezing Hill far to the north. *After going through a KG at the far end*, you may wish to carry on for a few metres to see an impressive cave – otherwise, *turn left immediately after going through the KG to follow a steep (and possibly slippery) track downhill beside the fence.*

Follow the track as it curves right, and, at the bottom, turn right for 15m before turning left down a stepped track. You may find fallen trees lying athwart the track, but carry on down in roughly the same direction until steps curve left to a broad path, down which you turn left. Carry on as the path curves up to the left before swinging right downhill. After negotiating rough stone steps, turn right across a stile (ST791662) *and follow a clear track across a field, heading to the left of a row of houses. After crossing another stile, turn left across a patch of grass and continue down a short road. At the bottom, bear*

1 Details can be found at *www.brownsfolly.org.uk*

right for a few metres, before turning down a footpath by Manor Farm Cottage.

St Swithun's church, which you pass on the left, was rebuilt in the 19th century with a grant from the Skrines of Warleigh Manor. Some fragments from the old church can be seen in the north wall. D'Oro House, which faces you at the bottom, is brand new. It stands in the former grounds of Bathford House, which was destroyed by fire in 1913. Only its stable block survived, and can be seen, now converted to a house, along to the left, beside the old gates to Bathford House.

The view from Browne's Folly

Cross the road and carry on down Ostlings Lane (originally known as Horselands Lane before being garbled into its present form over the years). *After turning right at the bottom, you have a choice:*

🚌 *To catch a bus back to Bath, carry on to the bus stop.*

To continue the walk, cross at the traffic island in front of the Crown Inn and turn left along the pavement. After crossing a footbridge over the By Brook, cross the road – patience is needed here – and, just before the railway bridge, turn left up a footpath (ST786670). *This takes you across the railway bridge, down the embankment on the other side and through a KG. Follow a track diagonally across the field, and, after going through a KG, climb steps to cross the railway line. Cross a stile on the far side and carry on along a lane. When you reach the canal, carry on along the towpath to head back into Bath.*

The Titfield Trilogy:
An Introduction

The quiet valleys explored in walks 10 to 12 were criss-crossed by a network of canals and railways, mostly built with one aim – to carry away coal from pits in the area. The main part of the Somerset coalfield lay further west, and it is only in walk 12 that the sites of some of the collieries are visited. Nevertheless, the canals and railways which served the coalfield had a profound impact on this area, and the earthworks associated with them remain one of its defining features today.

The first to be built was the Somersetshire Coal Canal (SCC). In 1792, as plans were being drawn up for a canal linking the Kennet with the Avon, a group of Somerset colliery owners drew up plans for another canal, which would branch off it at Monkton Combe. This canal was to run west along the valley of the Midford Brook to Midford, where it would divide. The northern arm would follow the valley of the Cam Brook to serve the collieries around Paulton, while the southern arm would run along the valley of the Wellow Brook to serve the collieries around Radstock.

Although this canal would be level as far as Midford, thereafter the land rose steeply and both arms of the canal would have to rise a considerable height before continuing westward. On the northern arm, where the canal had to be raised over 40m, it was decided, instead of building a flight of locks, to go for a more innovative solution, by trying out a 'Patent Hydrostatick or Caisson Lock' invented by Robert Weldon from Leicestershire. This consisted of a lift which would convey a 'caisson', over 20m long, and containing sufficient water to float a boat filled with coal, between the upper and lower levels. Access to the caisson was by means of doors at either end, which were sealed as it ascended or descended. The idea was ingenious, but fraught with difficulties from the start. The prodigious weight of a loaded caisson, the difficulty of ensuring a watertight seal, and the intractable nature of the clay and Fuller's Earth through which the shaft was constructed all told against it, and the project was eventually abandoned.

To bridge the gap between the upper and lower levels of the canal, an inclined plane was built, down which coal was transhipped from

Opposite: The Somerset & Dorset Railway viaduct at Midford, towering above the Camerton & Limpley Stoke Railway viaduct. This was the location for the opening sequence of *The Titfield Thunderbolt*. Both lines have now lain derelict for over half a century.

boats at the top to boats at the bottom. This was only a temporary measure, as work got under way to build a flight of 22 locks. Because of the lie of the land between the upper and lower levels, however, the flight could not head straight downhill, but had to curve round

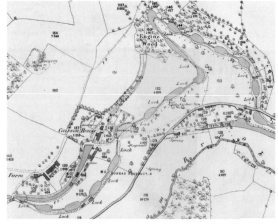

A late 19th-century OS map showing the flight of locks built to replace the caisson

the side of a hill before doubling back partway down.

As for the southern arm, this too was provided with an inclined plane linking the two levels. However, because of problems supplying water to the upper level, it was decided not to replace it with a flight of locks but to convert the whole of the southern arm to a horse-drawn tramway, from which coal was transhipped into boats at Midford.

Despite all these teething problems, both canal and tramway operated successfully for many years, and by the 1850s were serving no less than 23 collieries.

Then the railways came.

The arrival of the Great Western (GWR) in Bath in 1840 had little impact, but

The canal network around Bath in 1833. The Coal Canal appears as the 'Somerset Can' and the tramway as 'Radstock R Rd'. The map also shows the Dorset & Somerset Canal – which was never completed – branching off the Kennet & Avon west of Trowbridge, as well as a Bath to Bristol canal which was never built.

the opening of a line from Frome to Radstock in 1854 marked the beginning of the end. Traffic began leaching away, and in 1871 the tramway from Midford to Radstock was sold to the Somerset & Dorset Railway (S&D) who built part of their new line from Evercreech to Bath along its trackbed. Opened in 1874, this line was the final link in a route linking Bournemouth with Bristol and the Midlands, and, cutting as it did through some of the most challenging terrain in Somerset, it was prodigiously expensive to build, with soaring viaducts and long tunnels.

Two years later, in 1873, the GWR opened a line from Bristol to Radstock, via Hallatrow. In 1881, they built a branch from Hallatrow to Camerton, serving collieries hitherto served by the northern arm of the SCC. The SCC soldiered on for another 13 years, in the face of declining traffic and falling revenues, before going into receivership in 1894. After failing to find a buyer, it closed four years later.

There matters would probably have rested, had not work on a major new colliery started at Dunkerton, between Midford and Camerton, in 1903. The GWR bought the derelict canal and extended the Hallatrow-Camerton branch – along the bed of the canal where practicable – to the new colliery. It soon became clear that Dunkerton Colliery was set to become the biggest in Somerset, and the GWR responded by extending the line eastward, again using the bed of the canal where possible, to Limpley Stoke, where it joined their line from Bath to Westbury.

Passenger services were introduced on the Camerton & Limpley Stoke (C&LS) line in 1910, but withdrawn as a wartime economy measure less than five years later. They resumed in 1923, before being finally withdrawn in 1925, after which the line was used only for goods – as well as special trains for Monkton Combe School at the beginning and

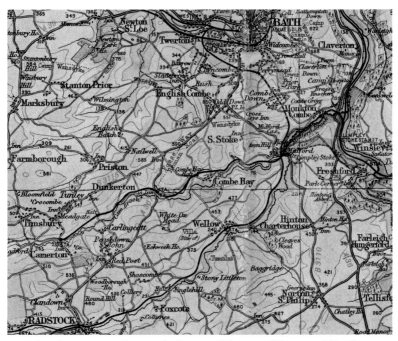

A early 20th-century map showing the Somerset & Dorset and Camerton & Limpley Stoke Railways

end of term. Dunkerton Colliery, which did indeed become the biggest in the Somerset coalfield – as well as the one with the worst reputation – also closed in 1925, after a working life of less than 20 years. Despite extraction being revived on a limited scale for a couple of years, and numerous reopening schemes, it soon fell silent forever. In 1932, with traffic on the C&LS line a shadow of what it had been a few years earlier, the GWR closed the line between Hallatrow and Camerton, retaining the Camerton-Limpley Stoke section to serve the surviving collieries in the area.

The last of the collieries along the line closed in 1950 and the line followed a year later. It would doubtless have faded into oblivion, had not fate devised one final role for this canal-turned-railway to play. Although built to carry coal, it ran through some of the most glorious countryside in England. Camerton station had already been used for a few short sequences in a film called *The Ghost Train*, based on a play by Arnold Ridley, back in 1931. Now, as the line sank into what should have been its final slumber, a crew from Ealing Studios, casting around for a ramshackle country railway, turned up to make what was destined to become one of the best-loved British films of all time.

The Titfield Thunderbolt is a stirring tale of how a group of villagers, appalled by the imminent closure of their local line, take it over and run it themselves, in the face of overwhelming odds and dastardly skulduggery. Filmed in the glorious summer of 1952, it was the line's swansong. There was to be no further reprieve. 'Titfield' was, as everyone knew from the start, an illusion, which lives on only in celluloid images over half a century old. The strange thing is, although the valley now echoes to the sound of 4x4s rather than 0-4-2 tank engines, and the

Filming at Monkton Combe station in the summer of 1952

railway is a distant memory, walking through this glorious and little changed corner of Somerset, the spirit of Titfield seems to live on.

With the final abandonment of the C&LS line, the only railway through the valley was the S&D. The opening sequence of *The Titfield Thunderbolt* features an S&D express speeding across Midford Viaduct while the Titfield Thunderbolt trundles through one of the arches below. At the time, the S&D was still part of an important north-south route, and the idea that it would close less than 14 years later would have seemed preposterous, yet, after through traffic was diverted onto other routes and services were reduced to a few dilatory local trains, the end, when it finally came on 6 March 1966, was a foregone conclusion. The S&D, steam-hauled to the end, is one of the most fondly remembered and bitterly missed lines in the country.

The S&D station at Midford today

In the three walks which follow, the Somersetshire Coal Canal, the Camerton & Limpley Stoke and the Somerset & Dorset Railways are encountered again and again. Walk 10 visits sites featured in *The Titfield Thunderbolt* before following the trackbed of the S&D from Midford to Bath; Walk 11 follows the towpath of the Coal Canal – and the route of the C&LS line – from Combe Hay to Tucking Mill; while Walk 12 visits the sites of collieries once served by canal and railway.

It goes without saying that there is no better introduction to these three walks, and to this glorious valley, than the film of *The Titfield Thunderbolt*. Watch it before you set off, and when you return, for it richly repays repeated viewings, and seeing how much or how little has changed is a fascinating exercise. You can, of course, buy the DVD online, but it is also available, along with books on the film, from a shop named after the film – The Titfield Thunderbolt Bookshop (titfield. co.uk), which can be found at 3a Upper Lambridge Street, Larkhall BA1 6RY, and is open Wednesday-Saturday, 10am-5.30pm.[1]

1 For more information, see Allsop, *The Somersetshire Coal Canal Rediscovered*; Atthill, *The Somerset & Dorset Railway*; Clew, *The Somersetshire Coal Canal & Railways*; Castens, *On the Trail of the Titfield Thunderbolt*; Elliott, *Queen of Waters*; Fosker, *The Titfield Thunderbolt Now & Then*; Macmillen & Chapman, *Coal from Camerton*; Maggs & Beale, *The Camerton Branch*.

The Titfield Trilogy: Walk 10
Return to Titfield

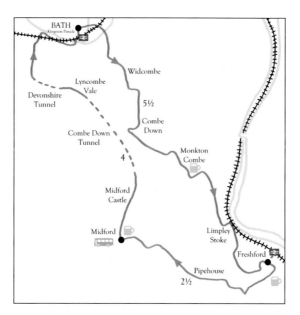

Distance: 12 miles;
    shorter options available by:
    catching a train from Freshford to Bath;
    or catching a bus (267) from Midford to Bath

Terrain: Mostly straightforward, although with some rough and muddy
    sections; sheep and cattle may be encountered at several points

Pubs and cafés:
    Wheelwrights Arms, Monkton Combe; lunch served 12-2 Mon-Fri,
    12-3 Sat & Sun (www.wheelwrightsarms.co.uk; 01225 722287)

    Inn at Freshford; food served all day Tue-Sat (sandwiches only 3-6
    weekdays), to 5pm Sun (theinnatfreshford.com; 01225 722250)

    Hope & Anchor, Midford; lunch served 12-2 Mon-Fri, 12-3 Sat &
    Sun (www.hopeandanchormidford.co.uk; 01225 832296)

Map: OS Explorer 155 & 142; or AA Walker's Map 25

Opposite: The bridge over the River Frome at Freshford

In this walk, we head via lanes and field paths up to Combe Down, before following drungways down to the village of Monkton Combe. After passing the site of Monkton Combe's railway station – renamed Titfield in the film – we climb through woods before dropping down to Limpley Stoke and heading south to Freshford, where there is an inn, as well as a station with regular trains back to Bath. From Freshford, we follow lanes and footpaths to Midford, where viaducts and bridges testify to this tiny village's former importance as a transport hub. It is here that we join the Two Tunnels Greenway, a shared path which follows the trackbed of the Somerset & Dorset (S&D) Railway back to Bath, passing Midford Castle, a striking 18th-century folly, before striding out across a lofty viaduct and plunging into a 1672m tunnel under Combe Down. Emerging in the sylvan seclusion of Lyncombe Vale, the path heads through a shorter tunnel, on the far side of which we leave the old line to head down paths and quiet roads to return to the city centre.

From Kingston Parade, head east along York Street. Turn right at the end and bear left by the Huntsman pub along North Parade. Cross at the lights, carry on along North Parade and cross at the lights at the end of North Parade Road. Turn right, take the second left up Pulteney Gardens, carry on across the canal bridge and, when the road forks, bear right uphill. Carry on past the turning to Abbey View Gardens, and, when the road forks again, bear right. At the end of The Tyning, cross and head along Church Street. This leads to the heart of old Widcombe, many of whose houses date from the 17th century, if not earlier.

When you reach the church, bear to the left of it along Church Lane. Carry on past the gates of Prior Park, and at the end bear left through a kissing gate (KG) beside a large metal gate and head up a track through a field. Here, less than a mile from the city centre, in a combe shelving gently uphill, surrounded by trees, with no houses visible and little if any noise beyond that of birdsong, you could be in the heart of the country.

Near the top of the field, go through a KG on the right, and follow a broad track alongside the hedgerow on your right. Carry straight on as it leads into a field and, when you meet a broad grassy track, bear left up it. At the top, go through a KG on the right and turn to take in one of the finest views of Bath, with Pulteney Bridge and weir at its centre.

Head on up to a KG, go through it and turn right uphill. After a few metres, by a stone wall, bear right. After 300m, when the path bears left alongside the fence around a playing field, carry straight on into woodland. The ground here is rough, with some steep declivities, the legacy of stone quarrying. Behind the high wall ahead lies a classical-style gymnasium built around 1839, when Prior Park was a Catholic seminary. To the right of it, two soaring beeches are perched on a high bank, their entwined and knotted roots exposed like some Tolkienesque fantasy of the Wildwood. *Head to the left of the wall, follow it as it turns south, go through a gate at the end, cross the road and turn right. After 200m, by the former Horseshoe pub, turn left along Tyning Road, and, a few metres along, turn left into Gladstone Road* (ST762626).

Beyond Beehive Cottage, at the end of a row of former quarrymen's cottages, the road dwindles to a drungway. After passing a house called Glenburnie, which boasts some of the finest ironwork in Bath, carry straight on along a road, with allotments on your left. When the road curves right into a school, carry on along a drungway on the left. This swings right through a broken KG before carrying on with the footings of a wall on the left and a high fence, screening deep quarries, on the right.

Carry on across a lane before bearing to the left of a large house, called Monkswold, and going through a KG. After 200m, another KG leads onto a road, where it is all but obligatory to stop to take in the view – there is even a handily-placed bench. Below, in the valley of the Midford Brook, lies the village of Monkton Combe. If you look eastward, to where the brook flows into the Avon, you will see a viaduct built in 1834 to carry the Warminster Road across the valley.

Heading down to Monkton Combe, with the Warminster Road viaduct visible on the left

Turn right and then immediately right again down another drungway (ST771622). At the bottom, *carry on along a road for 30m before following it round to the left. Just past the Wheelwright's Arms* 🍺*, turn right down Mill Lane.* Carry on past cottages bedecked with flowers, and, after passing an 18th-century lock-up, look out for two black metal gateposts flanking a garage on the left. This was the entrance to Monkton Combe station, which doubled as Titfield, and these posts are all that survives of it.

On the other side of the lane, the former trackbed, where Titfield's impromptu engine shed stood, is now

Top: A late 19th-century OS map showing the Coal Canal winding through Monkton Combe

Below: On this early 20th-century OS map, the canal has been replaced by the railway, although Canal Cottages still survive

Bottom: A photograph of the canal at Monkton Combe in the 1890s, with Canal Cottages in the background

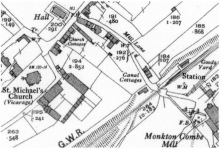

A train at Monkton Combe station, open to passengers for only seven years – from 1910 to 1915 and from 1923 to 1925

the driveway to a house. Before the railway was built, the Coal Canal ran along here, and the lane crossed it on a bridge. Looking uphill, you can see the lane down which, in the film, villagers are seen walking to the station. This scene is featured several times, along with two other shots of people heading for the station. You will look in vain for those other locations in Monkton Combe, though, as they were filmed a couple of miles away. You will, however, be seeing them later.

Carry on down the lane and continue along a footpath, passing Monkton Combe Mill on your left. This was a flock mill, where old clothes were broken down into flock for use in the upholstery trade. After the last of the collieries served by the railway closed in 1950, the only regular traffic on the line was to and from this mill, but it closed completely the following year when the mill was put up for sale. A brief revival came the following summer with the filming of *The Titfield Thunderbolt*, before final dereliction and the lifting of the rails in 1957.

Cross a footbridge, continue across another footbridge over the Midford Brook, and turn left across a step stile (ST774617). *When you come to a lane, turn left past Water House*, built for wealthy clothiers in the 17th century, and now a hotel. *When another lane trails in from the right, look across to the hedgerow on the right where you will see a stile* (ST776618). *Cross it and follow a track up through a meadow, before crossing another stile and heading up through the woods. Carry on as the track levels out and winds through the woods before crossing a clearing. After re-entering the woods, ignore a path forking left and carry on past a coppice maintained by the Heartwood Project.*

After passing large gates you come to the busy A36. Cross with care and head down the lane opposite. After 60m, follow a footpath sign through a gate on the right into a park. At the far end, go through another gate and turn left down a footpath. Carry straight on downhill and turn right along a lane at the bottom. After 400m, turn right up a footpath with steps (ST784606) *and carry on across a lane.* At the end you come to Limpley Stoke church, which dates back to Saxon times and lies on the parish and county boundary, some distance from the centre of the village.

Go through a squeeze stile to the right of the church and carry on through a KG. Do not take the track leading straight on, but bear left to follow one leading diagonally downhill. Follow it as it leads through a play area and past Freshford village shop and café, to emerge on a lane. Cross and bear left along a footpath veering away from the lane.

When you come to the war memorial (ST786599)*, turn left along a lane* commanding a good view of the village. *Turn left downhill at the end past the school and take the first right past the surgery.* Ahead on the right you will see the old Greyhound pub. The hanging sign dates from after it closed in 1957, but the ghost sign on its side wall is a genuine survival. At least three sets of lettering are visible, including one for the Freshford Brewery, which closed in 1894.

When the lane forks, bear right downhill and, after passing Avondale House, look up the lane beside it to see the old Freshford Brewery, still boasting an impressive chimney. *As the lane swings right, you pass the Old Parsonage* – home to Mr Valentine (played by Stanley Holloway) in *The Titfield Thunderbolt*. *Carry on uphill past the old fire engine house* and, when you come to the steps leading into the churchyard, turn round to look back down the hill. This is where one of those shots mentioned earlier, of villagers heading for Titfield station, was filmed. The other comes into view as you *carry on past the church and head downhill.*

Looking down the hill from Freshford church, with the old brewery on the right and the Old Parsonage – Mr Valentine's house in *The Titfield Thunderbolt* – in front of it

Freshford's station – unlike Monkton Combe's – is still open, so *if you want to end the walk here, take the first left and walk along to the station, which has an hourly service back to Bath.*

If you carry on downhill, however, you will come to the Inn at Freshford 🍺*, where you can enjoy a well-earned break before either heading back to the station or continuing with the walk.*

Although no tourist honeypot, Freshford is one of the most delightfully situated and attractive villages in Somerset. For centuries it was also one of the wealthiest. Sheep grazing its broad meadows produced wool which was turned into cloth in mills powered by the fast-flowing River Frome. So grand were the houses built by the mill owners that John Wood thought they looked 'like a Collection of little Palaces'. Writing later in the 18th century, Edmund Rack described Freshford,

> both with respect to its buildings and situation, as pleasant as most little towns in this county, having some elegant and many good houses inhabited by gentlemen and considerable clothiers. Its situation is on the southern declivity of a hill in a part of the country well cultivated and which a pleasing intermixture of hills, woods, deep valleys and glens have rendered very picturesque and romantic ... The river Avon washes this town on the east where it is joined by a stream which rises near Frome over which is a stone bridge of three arches erected in the year 1783. Both these rivers contain trout, eels, perch, pike, roach and dace.

Today, although sheep still graze the fields around the village, the mills have long fallen silent, converted to provide housing for some of those who want to live in this enviably located rural bolthole.[1]

On leaving the inn, carry on across the bridge, go through a KG 100m along on the right and head across a large field. On the right you will see a red-brick pillbox, built in 1940 as part of a defence line to protect Bristol in the event of a German invasion. As you carry on, two of Freshford's grander houses come into view. To your left is Freshford Hall,

The Hermitage

built around 1790, with wings added around 1885, while high up on the right is the Hermitage, dating from medieval times but much altered.

1 For more on Freshford, see Dodge, *The History of a Somerset Village.*

After going through a KG on the far side of the field (ST787597), *turn right along a lane and follow it as it swings left alongside the river.* On the far bank is another pillbox. The large house above it is called Abbotsleigh and dates from the 1830s. On your left is Freshford Mill. After closing in the 1930s, it became a rubber factory, which ceased production in 1995. The site is now being converted to housing. If you look to the left when you come to a bridge, you can glimpse (unless it

THE GHQ GREEN LINE

After the evacuation of British troops from Dunkirk in May 1940, General Sir Edmund Ironside, who was in charge of Britain's land defences, ordered the creation of a series of GHQ (General Head-quarters) defence lines across the country, following pre-existing obstacles such as rivers or canals. Pillboxes, from which machine guns or anti-tank guns could be fired at invading forces, were built at regular intervals along them, with the aim of impeding an enemy invasion.

When Ironside was promoted shortly afterwards, his place was taken by General Alan Brooke, who believed that defence 'should be of a far more mobile and offensive nature'. Ironside's plan for an extensive network of fixed defences was scaled down before being finally abandoned in 1941. Nevertheless, it has left a lasting legacy, as many of the pillboxes, designed to withstand heavy bombardment, have, not surprisingly, stood the test of time.

Pillbox beside the River Frome at Freshford

The GHQ Lines were colour coded; these pillboxes form part of the Green Line which ran from Highbridge to Bradford on Avon, from where the Blue Line ran along the Kennet & Avon Canal to Reading. The Green Line, meanwhile, continued north to Malmesbury, before bearing north-east through Avening to Framilode on the River Severn, thus – in theory – providing an outer ring of defence for Bristol and Avonmouth.

has been hidden by redevelopment) the shell of a 16th-century building at the heart of the mill.

After crossing the bridge, follow the lane as it swings left. When you come to a T junction, go through a KG on the right, head up a footpath with

The shell of a 16th-century building – now being redeveloped – at the heart of Freshford Mill

steps and go through another KG at the top. If you turn right along the lane for 25m, there is a splendid view south along the Frome valley, with the Westbury White Horse in the distance.

To continue the walk, however, you want to head in the other direction, past Abbotsleigh. Just beyond Abbotsleigh, you pass another of Freshford's lost pubs, the Golden Lion, on your right. *Turn right at the end by Abbotsleigh Coach House. When you come to a T junction at the top, bear right past Abbey Cottage.* Dolphin House, a little way along on the left, is yet another lost pub.

Take the next turning left up Pipehouse Lane (ST781598) *and, after crossing the busy A36, carry on along the lane to Pipehouse. After passing Turnip Wood Cottage, the lane – an old packhorse route – becomes a muddy byway, with views south-westward over the valley*

Looking along the Frome valley, with the Westbury White Horse in the distance

149

of the Wellow Brook to the Mendips. After 800m, as the byway starts to descend, the views improve, but the track deterio-rates. Unless it has recently been repaired, you will find that parts have been gouged away by torrential rain and care is needed as you pick your way down it. *Carry on as the byway swings right up-hill before drop-ping down to a busy road. Cross over to a build-ing with an arch-way – once the Fox Inn – and turn left along*

The view over the valley of the Wellow Brook

Heading down to Midford

the pavement for 30m, before turning right across a footbridge by Midford Mill (ST763606). *Go through a KG and head across a field, keeping to the right of a raised strip.*

Cross a stile by the stream and head towards a viaduct that once carried the S&D. Below it are the remains of another viaduct which carried the Camerton & Limpley Stoke (C&LS) line, and was where the opening sequence of *The Titfield Thunderbolt* was filmed (ST760605).

Turn right along a lane beside the S&D viaduct. The metal bridge a little way along crossed the Coal Canal, whose course the C&LS line had diverged from by this point. If you look to the right when you reach the main road, you will see the Hope & Anchor pub 🍺, once a canalside tavern.

🚌 *There is also, if you want to cut short the walk at this point, a bus stop with regular services back to Bath on the opposite side of the road to the pub.*

To carry on, cross the main road and turn left for a few metres, before turning right up the Old Midford Road and right again into the pub car park, on the far side of which is what remains of the S&D's Midford station. This closed, along with the rest of the line, in 1966.

Head along the trackbed past the platform of Midford station, and carry on

Walking along the trackbed near Tucking Mill

along the line. After you pass through a short tunnel, Midford Castle comes into view on your left. It was built around 1775 with a ground plan based on the ace of clubs, which has given rise to all manner of tall stories to account for its origin. More recently it was owned by the actor Nicholas Cage.

Before long, you find your-self striding out across Tucking Mill viaduct. When the S&D opened in 1874, the viaduct was single track, but in 1903, as part of plans to upgrade the line, it was widened so that another track could be laid. The plans were abandoned, however, and despite the work having been carried out, the line across the viaduct remained single to the end. In 2013, after being sealed off for almost 50 years, the viaduct reopened as part of the Two Tunnels Greenway.

After passing through a cutting with arches shoring up unstable ground, you enter the first of those two tunnels. Combe Down Tunnel was, at 1672m, the longest in the country without ventilation shafts. It was also single track and, for

Widening Tucking Mill Viaduct in 1903

MIDFORD CASTLE: A DIFFERENCE OF OPINION

'A transient glance at Midford Castle would immediately recall to the English traveller's remembrance Eaglehurst, in Hampshire. The surrounding landscape resembles as much as is natural that about Tivoli; the rocks are no bad substitutes for ruins, and a contemplative eye may wander from the terrace at Midford Castle, till the imagination is transported into Italy. The solemn gloom of this enchanted spot is accompanied by a repose and silence in perfect harmony with it. The murmur of an indistinct echo, produced by a small but picturesque waterfall in the vale beneath, the tinkling of a bell, or the barking of a dog, reverberated from rock to rock, are all the sounds that intrude on this abode of contemplation.'

From *A Picturesque Guide to Bath, &c* by Ibbetson et al, 1793

'Midford Castle, as it is called, [is] an anomaly in building, equally at war with taste and comfort. This edifice, without back or front, beginning or end, would form a triangle, were not the corners rounded off into towers, which, with its embattled top, Gothic windows, and bastion on the lower side, suggested, with sufficient impropriety, the proud name which it at present bears. Much money has doubtless been expended on its erection, and it would be difficult to find an instance where expense has been so injudiciously bestowed; since its plan at once excludes beauty and convenience. Every advantage of situation it may fairly boast; a broad extent of valley spreads itself to the right, bounded by distant hills; a river and a village lie immediately below it; and to the left the eye wanders with rapture through a deep winding dale, darkened with woods, and diversified with rock and precipice. How may we lament, that when Art attempted anything in a scene for which Nature had done so much, she did not work with the tools of Taste!'

From *Excursions from Bath* by the Rev Richard Warner, 1801

A southbound express crossing Tucking Mill Viaduct in the 1930s

most of its length, had a gradient of 1 in 100, so that heavily-loaded northbound trains had to work flat out, pumping it full of smoke. It could, quite literally, be deadly. In November 1929, the driver and fireman of a northbound goods train were overcome by fumes, and, as the train breasted the summit and began the descent towards Bath, were unable to halt its headlong progress. It eventually derailed as it approached the station, killing the driver and two railway workers in the yard.

Eventually, you emerge into Lyncombe Vale, a sylvan interlude before the 409m-long Devonshire Tunnel, on a gradient of 1 in 50 – downhill heading north but a punishing and smoky climb for trains heading south.

Shortly after leaving Devonshire Tunnel, turn right by a five-bar gate, head along a path and turn left at a T junction. Turn right when you come to a road, and carry on as the road curves (ignoring a turning with No Entry signs on the right and a turning to Maple Gardens on the left), before taking the second turning on the left. At a T junction, with a half-timbered building on your left, cross and turn right for a few metres, before turning left down a footpath just past the gates of Lyncombe Rectory. When you come to a road, cross and carry on down another footpath. At the next road, turn right, carry on under a railway bridge and turn right along the Lower Bristol Road, crossing the river at the end to return to the city centre.

The Titfield Trilogy: Walk 11
Along the Coal Canal

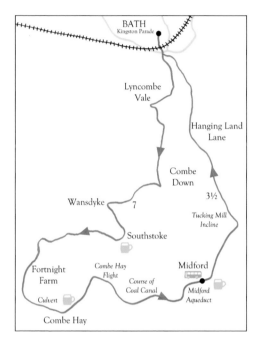

Distance: 10½ miles;
  shorter option by catching a bus (267) from Midford to Bath

Terrain: Generally straightforward, although with possible muddy sections; a torch is recommended for negotiating the culvert under the canal; sheep and cattle may be encountered at various points

Pubs and cafés:
  Packhorse, Southstoke; due to reopen 2018 (packhorsebath.co.uk)

  Wheatsheaf, Combe Hay; lunch served 12-2 Mon-Fri, 12-2.30 Sun (www.wheatsheafcombehay.com; 01225 833504)

  Hope & Anchor, Midford; lunch served 12-2 Mon-Fri, 12-3 Sat & Sun (www.hopeandanchormidford.co.uk; 01225 832296)

Map: OS Explorer 155 & 142; or AA Walker's Map 25

Opposite: Horsecombe Vale from Shepherds Walk

After heading out of Bath along Lyncombe Vale, this walk follows an old road up to Combe Down before heading to the village of Southstoke, from where there are superb views southward. After following footpaths down to the valley of the Cam Brook, we negotiate a 50m culvert through an embankment which carried the Somersetshire Coal Canal (SCC) and later the Camerton & Limpley Stoke Railway (C&LSR). Then comes the highlight of the walk, as we join a path winding downhill past a ruinous but spectacular flight of locks, before following the old canal towpath to Midford.

The Coal Canal is best remembered today for the man hired to survey the route, William Smith. Observing the different layers of rocks through which the canal was cut, he developed the theory of stratification, which became the foundation of modern geology. Continuing along the towpath from Midford to Tucking Mill, we visit the canalside house where he lived, before climbing a path which follows the course of an inclined plane he built to bring stone down from a quarry. After carrying on uphill via a series of drungways to Combe Down, the walk ends by following another old road, little changed for centuries, back to the city.

From Kingston Parade, head east along York Street. Turn right at the end, bear left by the Huntsman pub along North Parade and then right along Pierrepont Street. Continue along Manvers Street and at the end go through a tunnel to the left of the railway station. Carry on across a footbridge over the river, cross two sets of pedestrian lights straight ahead, bear right for a few metres, then turn left up Lyncombe Hill.

After 500m, when the road curves right, take the second turning on the left down Lyncombe Vale Road. At the bottom of the hill, as the road curves left, bear right to continue along Lyncombe Vale Road. After 200m, follow a footpath sign up steps on the left. After a crosspath, continue up more steps before following the path as it curves left alongside a fence. When you come to a bridge over the trackbed of the Somerset & Dorset (S&D) Railway – now the Two Tunnels Greenway – turn right across it (ST752634). *After going through a gate, follow a track bearing slightly to the left up a field.*

Go through a gate at the top and turn left along a lane. After 150m, when you come to a gatepost for Foxhill Grove, turn right uphill. For a while, you can enjoy the sylvan beauty of this old lane, until, after passing bollards, it levels out, passing an old MOD site – now being redeveloped – on the left.

At the main road, cross and carry straight on along Cleevedale Road. After 250m, as the road starts to curve left, bear right along a footpath known as Shepherds Walk (ST753621), which commands superb views over Horsecombe Vale. ***Carry on across the end of a cul de sac, and at the end cross the road and turn left to walk along to the Cross Keys pub,*** built around three hundred years ago and possibly incorporating an even older building.

After crossing the main road, go up steps beside the bus stop and turn right through a squeeze stile to follow the course of the defensive earthwork known as the Wansdyke.[1] After 350m, turn left through a kissing gate (KG) to follow a track beside a wall. Carry on in the same direction, and, when you come to a drive, carry on through a KG and alongside another wall before turning right down a lane. Just past Pound Cottage, look to your right to see a declivitous outcrop of oolitic limestone.

As you carry on, the lane opens out and the village of Southstoke lies below you. To your left stood Southstoke Brewery, which closed around 1907 and was later demolished, although Brewery House and Brewery Cottage still survive,

Southstoke village c1910

The Packhorse Inn

as do the roadside vaults where barrels were once stored. The lane ahead leads down to the Packhorse Inn 🍺, a glorious old building with a datestone of 1674, although it is thought it may be even older. After closing in 2012, it was bought by a new owner who planned to turn it into a private house. In response, the villagers launched a campaign to save it, and, after a long struggle, acquired it in 2016. Since then, they

1 For more on the Wansdyke, see pages 174-5

have started the long and costly process of refurbishment. Although not yet open at time of publication, some successful open days have already been held, with local beer and cider flowing again, and a grand reopening is eagerly anticipated. The spirit of Titfield lives on!

To continue the walk, bear right and, after passing the church lych-gate, follow a footpath sign through a KG beside a five-bar gate. **After passing Manor Farm,** whose 15th-century tithe barn incorporates a spectacular dovecote, *bear right uphill when the track forks.* At the top of the rise, a toposcope was set up in 2000, commanding a view which extends from Pen Hill in the west to Westbury White Horse in the east. From here, on a clear day, you can also see the Silbury-like profile of Cley Hill and no less than three grand follies – Cranmore Tower, Ammerdown Column and Alfred's Tower at Stourhead. *Carry on along the track, which eventually dwindles to a narrow path. Continue through a KG, passing fields on the right renamed Sulis Down, where developers have applied to build 173 homes. After going through a KG at the end, turn sharp left down*

Southstoke tithe barn c1910

The view from the toposcope

a rough track, before immediately bearing right down a holloway with a footpath sign (ST733612).

Go through a gate and head downhill with the fence on your left. At the bottom, go through a KG and a handgate and bear right along a farm track. After 250m, you pass Fortnight Farm on the right. Carry on for 300m, before following a footpath sign across a stile on the left. The building you can see over to your right is Week Farm. A little further along the track is Three Days Cottage. Apparently, the reason for these names is that the buildings were part of an estate, and each had to provide sufficient produce to maintain the estate for a given period each year.

Having crossed the stile, follow a track alongside a fence which, after a few metres, bears right alongside a brook. After the track enters woodland, you will see that the way ahead is blocked by a high

Heading down to Combe Hay

Emerging from the culvert at Combe Hay

embankment which originally carried the SCC, and later the C&LSR.

There is a way through the embankment by means of a subway – or culvert – which the footpath shares with the brook (ST732602). *The footpath follows a broken-down causeway in the*

centre of the culvert which should be reasonably dry if there has not been much rain, but may be impassable in the rainy season. Even if it is dry, a torch is advisable.

● *If you decide not to attempt the culvert, bear right alongside the embankment, continue along a farm track and turn left when you come to a lane. After crossing an old railway bridge a few metres along, turn left to follow a lane through the village of Combe Hay. As you leave the village, passing the Wheatsheaf pub* 🍺 *on your left, skip the next paragraph, and pick up the directions in the following one.*

● *If you do go through the culvert, after re-emerging at the far end, follow the track as it crosses and winds alongside the brook, splitting into two at one point before joining up again.* On a sunny spring day, with the banks covered in wild garlic, this section is a delight, especially after the echoing dankness of the culvert. *Carry on across a stile, and, after climbing some steps, bear right and right again down a lane, passing the Wheatsheaf pub* 🍺 *on your left, and turning left along the lane at the bottom.*

● *When the lane forks, bear left (following a No Through Road sign) and cross an old railway bridge* (ST738601). This is Barningham's Bridge, which featured twice in *The Titfield Thunderbolt* – in the race between the train and Pearce & Crump's bus, and in the final triumphant run, with the veteran locomotive *Lion* hauling Dan's coach, whose chimney has to be lowered to pass under the bridge.

Carry on up the lane past Rowley Farm. When a gate blocks the way ahead, turn right through a KG and head straight down a field. Just before a gate at the bottom, turn left along a narrow path through scrub. On your left are the remains of a feeder canal which supplied water to a pump house, an arch of which survives a little further along. *Follow a path to the right of it, which heads steeply downhill beneath tall beeches and may be slippery.* If you look down to your right you will see part of the derelict flight of locks. The pump house was built to draw up water lost when boats passed through them.

Follow the path as it curves to the right round a dried-up basin where the flight of locks executed an oblique change of direction. Negotiating this tight curve was a tricky business, and boatmen dubbed it the bull's nose. *Carry on down past five locks.* The first is overgrown and in a dangerous state but the others have recently been cleared of vegetation. *At the end, cross a stile and go under a railway bridge.* This bridge also features in *The Titfield Thunderbolt*, when Pearce & Crump's bus comes to a screeching halt as it encounters an oncoming car, while the Titfield Thunderbolt steams blithely by above.

Cross the lane, go through a KG on the other side and continue alongside a paddock. You are still following the course of the canal, although here it has been filled in. The stone abutment you pass on the left, 300m along, was where Fuller's Earth, mined in the hills above, was brought down to the canal to be loaded into barges. Just past it, ***follow steps up to a gate*** (ST748602).

The bottom lock on the Combe Hay flight

A bridge over the dried-up canal

There was a bridge over the canal here, but it collapsed in the 1970s. As you go through the gate, look straight ahead to see a medieval packhorse route leading uphill, its course blocked by the railway embankment.

Turn right and, after a few metres, go through a gate on the left to continue along the old towpath. Evidence of the canal, with more abandoned locks, soon appears. *Follow the towpath for 1000m, but, when the way ahead is blocked by the railway embankment, go through a gate, turn right and follow a path under a viaduct to rejoin the canal on the other side.*

After passing an old canal bridge, look to the right to see a recently-restored aqueduct crossing the brook (ST758605). This carried the southern arm of the canal to a basin at the foot of the inclined plane down which came coal from the pits around Radstock.

Above: The dried-up canal bed between Combe Hay and Midford

Below: The railway viaduct over the Cam Brook

Bottom: The aqueduct which carried the southern arm of the canal across the Cam Brook

Carry on through a wooden KG, passing a bog garden established on the bed of the canal. *Go under a metal road bridge and a viaduct which once carried the S&D Railway, to emerge onto a busy road.*

If you want to return to Bath by bus from here, there is a bus stop just along to the right.

Otherwise, cross to the Hope & Anchor 🍺 and turn right. Just past the pub, you come to the parapet of a bridge which crossed the canal. *After passing a house called The Moorings, turn left along a footpath. A few metres further on, the footpath curves right past a fence*, behind which stood a building which weighed boats, together with their cargoes, to assess how much toll had to be paid. *The path soon curves back to follow the course of the towpath*, with the S&D embankment high above. This is one

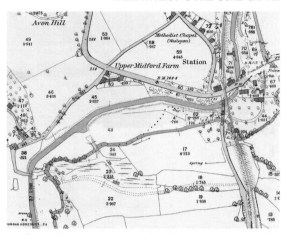

A late 19th-century OS map of Midford showing the Coal Canal and the Somerset & Dorset Railway

By the time of this early 20th-century map, the canal had been abandoned and the Camerton & Limpley Stoke line built

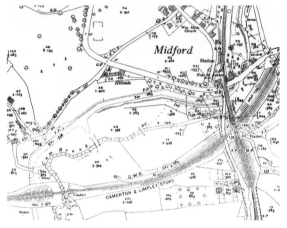

of the most picturesque stretches of the old canal, especially in spring, when first celandines and then wild garlic bloom where coal-blackened waters once flowed. *After 400m, though, all semblance of the canal disappears, as the path curves alongside a lane and goes through a KG. The canal bed has been filled in beyond this point, and, as you carry on, the path drops down to run below the embankment, before leading onto the lane.*

Opposite, you will see a former canalside cottage with Gothic windows and a plaque to William Smith, 'the Father of English Geology', which was unveiled by the Bath Natural History & Antiquarian Field Club in 1889. Unfortunately, it is on the wrong house. To see where

William Smith lived, you need to **turn right along the lane for 50m to Tucking Mill House** (ST766615). Although the mistake has long been known, and there have been repeated calls for the plaque to be moved, so far it remains where it was originally – and erroneously – unveiled.[1]

The old towpath between Midford and Tucking Mill

In 1801, the Rev Richard Warner rode along the towpath here, and left this account of his journey:

> The canal, cut along the side of the hill, runs nearly parallel with the river a considerable distance down the vale, and will soon afford a ride for some miles of exquisite beauty; amongst the little rural scenes and interesting objects it offers, is Tucker-mill [sic], a cottage crouching under the high bank that rises above it, and seen from the Midford road, the residence of Mr Smith. Professing to point out everything remarkable in our route, it would be unpardonable in me to pass by the mansion, though it be a lowly one, of a man ... whose invincible industry and indefatigable perseverance, unaided by the advantages of fortune or situation, have furnished him with a degree of geological and mineralogical knowledge which few, if any, of his contemporaries possess. Patient observation and practical experience, blended with great natural sagacity, have enabled him to form a system, of geology equally new and satisfactory, which, you will hear with pleasure, is intended for the world, when properly digested and arranged.

Warner's reference to a 'cottage' may have been the reason the plaque was placed on the wrong house. No doubt accustomed to grander abodes, he may well have considered Tucking Mill House no more than a cottage, but his description of it 'crouching under the

1 See Eyles, 'William Smith's Home Near Bath'.

Left: The house on which the plaque to William Smith was unveiled

Opposite page: The house where he is now known to have lived

Below: The path following the course of Smith's tramway

Above: A fragment of rail on the old tramway

high bank that rises above it' makes it clear that this is the building he is referring to.

Just past the house, turn left up a footpath, which follows the course of an inclined plane built by William Smith to carry stone down to the canal. Work on it started around 1811, but it was abandoned less than ten years later. Fragments of rails and stone sleepers can still be seen along the path, and a short length of rail, which may have come from the plane, is in use as a post on steps behind the house.[1] As you continue to climb, you can see Tucking Mill Reservoir, and beyond it the S&D viaduct spanning Horsecombe Vale. *After going through a KG, you will see the S&D – now the Two Tunnels Greenway – in a cutting to your left. Carry on through a KG and continue uphill, passing another KG.* To your left is the former Combe Down Paper Mill, built in 1805 by the 2nd Baron de Montalt. It produced high quality writing paper, drawing paper used by Turner and Constable, and paper for bank notes. It was powered by a waterwheel 17m in diameter – said to be the largest in England – as well as by a steam engine. By 1834, it had gone over to the production of gutta percha, and later became a cabinet works, before being converted to housing.

The view through Pope's Arch

Carry on up a flight of steps beside a spring and continue up a drungway. At a road, turn left for a few metres before turning right up another drungway. At the next road, cross and carry on along a level drungway, which leads past a succession of back gardens. At the end, bear left to cross to the Hadley Arms, then turn right across the main road. Head to the left of a gatepost and bear left along a drungway.

Although initially it may not seem that exciting, this is arguably the finest way to approach Bath on foot. After 300m, you come to a stone on the right marking the boundary of Lyncombe & Widcombe, which is believed to stand on the spot where a moot or meeting tree stood in Saxon times (ST758628). A little further on, you go under a grotto-like bridge, built by Ralph Allen to carry a private drive over the path, and

1 See Pollard, 'Bath Stone Quarry Railways'

THE LYNCOMBE MOOT-TREE

'Our history north and south of the Avon becomes unified under Alfred the Great, and there is interesting work to be done among our place-names, in tracing how the artificially named *tons* of Saxon organisation ... have sometimes remained and sometimes slipped back to their more British *combes*, *pens* and *lyns*. In one of our Saxon charters, especially, we have proof of the artificial naming that took place, and of the relapse to a British name; for the great estate of *Lyncombe* was granted to the Monastery by King Edgar as *Cliftune*, the one name pure British, the other pure Saxon; and it is the British name which is found surviving in Domesday Book and to the present day ... In the Cliftune-Lyncombe charter one of the boundaries takes us straight to the moot-tree of the tunship, or group of tunships that are close together there. The *Tunnes Treow* it is called. Who has ever heard of any other place  that has a Saxon charter which indicates the exact spot where an ancient moot-tree stood? Yet Bath has done no more for this historic spot than to print a translation and interpretation of these boundaries that makes the *tunnes treow* – a gallows! The charter is Nº 25 in our Bath Cartulary and the site of the tun's tree is at the top of the 'hanging land' of Blind Lane, by Prior Park, where the Widcombe boundary stone stands.'

From 'The History of Bath: Unexplored Sources and Fresh Records, Part III', by Mrs EW Symons, *Bath Chronicle*, 13 August 1927

known as Pope's Arch, because of the poet Alexander Pope's connection with Prior Park. Once through it, the scene changes dramatically. This lane has a variety of names – Blind Lane, Pope's Walk, and, perhaps most evocatively, Hanging Land Lane. As the lane steepens, the city of Bath is glimpsed through the trees, and you get an inkling of what it would have been like to enter the city in the mid-16th century, as John Leland did, 'down by a rocky hill full of fair springs of water'.

After passing the Roman Catholic cemetery, with its two Gothic-style mortuary chapels, turn right by the gateway to The Cloisters, and at the end turn left down Prior Park Road. You will notice that, although you are now fast approaching the city, there are still fields and orchards on the left, while the car showroom on your right was, until the 1920s, a mill. *At the end, by the White Hart, turn left, carry on to the traffic lights you crossed near the start of the walk and retrace your steps to the city centre.*

The Titfield Trilogy: Walk 12
Over the Wansdyke to Coal Country

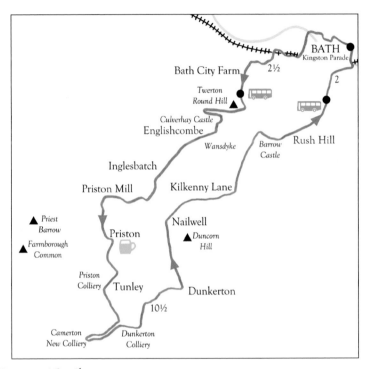

Distance: 15 miles;
  shorter options available by:
  catching a bus (1) to Twerton Round Hill at the start;
  catching a bus (4) from Bloomfield Drive to Bath at the end

Terrain: Generally straightforward, although with possible muddy
  sections; sheep and cattle may be encountered at various points

Pubs and cafés:
  Ring O'Bells, Priston; lunch served Fri-Sun 12-3, closed Mon-Thu
  lunchtimes (www.priston.org.uk/ringobells.htm; 01761 471467)

Map: OS Explorer 155 & 142; or AA Walker's Map 25

Opposite: Mill Lane, between Inglesbatch and Priston Mill

Round hills – both natural and artificial – are encountered several times in this walk, which heads south-west from the city into a land of undulating fields and green lanes. We climb first to Twerton Round Hill – long believed to be man-made – before dropping down past the forlorn ruins of a Norman castle to a village with the evocative name of Englishcombe. After crossing the enigmatic earthwork known as the Wansdyke, we head into some of the quietest and most delectable countryside around Bath, passing within sight of two more round hills, before stepping stones lead across the Conygre Brook to Priston Mill. Then comes Priston village – and the Ring o'Bells pub – before we head south into coal country, and round hills of a very different stamp – the grass-covered batches (or slag heaps) of long-closed collieries. After following the course of the Coal Canal and railway to Dunkerton, we head back to Bath, along winding lanes and hidden paths, with distant glimpses of the city's upper terraces across the fields.

From Kingston Parade, head to the left of the Abbey, cross Abbey Church Yard, and, after passing under the colonnade, turn right along Stall Street. Turn left along Westgate Street and cross into Kingsmead Square at the end. On the far side of the square, head along New Street and turn right along James Street West. At the crossroads, turn right up Charles Street, cross at the pedestrian lights partway up and carry straight on along New King Street.

Take the second right along Nile Street, turn left along the Upper Bristol Road, and after 250m turn left along Victoria Bridge Road. Head over the bridge and carry on, crossing the Lower Bristol Road and heading up Brougham Hayes. After 300m, just before the railway bridge, turn right down steps to follow a path alongside the line.

After passing Oldfield Park station, cross Brook Road and carry on along a footpath which soon curves away from the line to emerge in Bellotts Road, which you cross to head along another footpath by a garage. Carry on when you come to a road, with Twerton Cemetery on your left, but, as the road curves, cross to go past wooden posts onto the Two Tunnels Greenway and bear left (ST733646). After crossing a railway bridge, bear right at a crosspath into a housing estate.

After 50m, bear left towards garages and then right along King George's Road. At the end, turn left up Lansdown View, and, when you come to Shophouse Road, with the White Horse pub ahead, turn right downhill. Shortly after passing Innox Road on the left, turn left through a kissing gate (KG) into Innox Park and bear left uphill beside the hedge (ST728644). When you reach the top corner of the field, you have a choice.

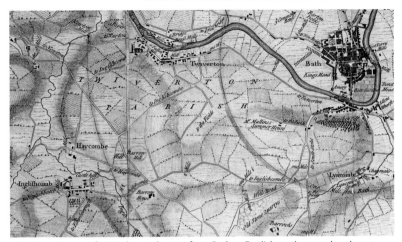

As Thorpe's map of 1742 shows, the way from Bath to Englishcombe once lay almost entirely though fields

The view over the city from Bath City Farm

● *If you want the quickest route, or if you have a dog with you, carry straight on up the path ahead, turn left along a road at the top, and skip the next paragraph.*

● *Otherwise, bear right alongside the hedge and, after passing a couple of benches, follow a path into woodland and go through a double KG on the left into Twerton City Farm. Head up through a sheep field (where dogs are not permitted), go through a wooden gate in the fence ahead and continue through a KG, passing a variety of animals. After going through a gate at the top, turn left, bear right before the buildings to follow a gravel track up to the road and turn left.*

The view over Twerton from Bath City Farm

● *At the T junction at the end of the road, turn right uphill. At the mini-roundabout by the Beehive Surgery – once the Beehive pub – turn left along Mount Road. At the next mini-roundabout, bear right and after 120m turn right to climb Twerton Round Hill.*

🚌 *If you have caught the bus from the city centre, get off at the stop for Twerton Round Hill and walk to the top of the hill.*

Looking west from Twerton Round Hill to the tower of Englishcombe church and the green hills beyond, you can survey the terrain you will be covering in this walk. There could not be a greater contrast with the view that greets you after climbing the hills to the north, east and south of the city. There, on reaching the edge of the escarpment, the plateau extends unrelievedly ahead; here the land folds enticingly away in true West Country fashion. It could be said that this is where the West Country really starts, and, as we shall see, after the Romans left and new colonisers arrived, it was for a time – we do not know how long – a borderland between the Saxons and the Romano-British.

The two rows of modern houses on the road below stand on the site of the Jubilee Inn, which closed in 2008 and burned down in 2011. Head down towards them, cross the road and turn right. Just before the garden centre turn left down Haycombe Lane (ST723632). The double gates you pass on the left, 200m down the lane, block what was for centuries one of two lanes linking Bath with Englishcombe – it can be clearly seen, for instance, on Thorpe's 1742 map on page 171. Known as Washpool Lane, this end of it was blocked in the late 20th century. To get to the part of it which is still a right of way, you need to make a long – if delightful – diversion.

A little further along the lane, look through a gap in the hedge to see the humps and bumps marking the site of Culverhay Castle across the valley. As the lane slowly descends, leaving Bath behind, trees arch overhead and the noise of traffic recedes. *After another 500m, turn left following a footpath sign towards Inglescombe Farm. Once past the farm, where there is a choice of footpaths, continue straight on, heading back in the direction of Twerton Round Hill. Carry on along a farm track, with views across to Culverhay Castle, but, when it curves*

Near Inglescombe Farm

The site of Culverhay Castle

uphill, follow a footpath sign along a narrow path straight ahead to emerge on Washpool Lane (ST720632).

THE MYSTERY OF THE WANSDYKE

Walls or ramparts built for defence or demarcation of territory are nothing new: the Romans built two to mark the limit of their empire in the north of Britain, and in the 8th century Offa built one to show where Powys ended and Mercia began. In our own time, building walls to keep people apart is more popular than ever. But the Wansdyke remains an intractable mystery. It was built sometime after the Romans left Britain, so, compared with Stonehenge, for example, it is relatively recent. But, whereas we now know a good deal about Stonehenge, we know next to nothing about the Wansdyke.

We know, in fact, less than was known – or was thought to be known – a century ago. In 1926, a sumptuously illustrated, meticulously researched book by Albany F Major and Edward J Burrow, called *The Mystery of Wansdyke*, was published. It described an earthwork starting near Portbury on the Bristol Channel, running through the hillforts of Maes Knoll and Stantonbury, past Englishcombe and across Bathampton Down, before dropping to the Avon valley north of Claverton. On the other side of the Avon, it followed the course of a Roman road eastward to Morgan's Hill, south of Calne, beyond which some truly monumental earthworks led across the Marlborough Downs towards Savernake Forest, where it seemed to peter out. Major and Burrow were far from being iconoclasts and, in mapping the route of the Wansdyke, they were following the consensus of opinion at the time.

Today, there is far less consensus concerning the Wansdyke, although the theory that it was conceived and built as a single entity, stretching halfway across southern England, is largely discredited. The concept of a western Wansdyke, starting not at Portbury but at Maes Knoll, north of Pensford, and ending at Odd Down, just east of Englishcombe, is gaining increased currency, along with the concept of an unrelated eastern Wansdyke running across the Marlborough Downs east of Morgan's Hill. The notion, indeed the very existence, of a central Wansdyke, linking the western and eastern sections by following the course of the Roman road, is now considered dubious. As for the western and eastern sections bearing the same name, this is almost certainly a red herring, as the name – derived from 'Woden's Dyke' – was only bestowed centuries later.

All the theories and conjectures, past and present, however, are based solely on the evidence – or lack of it – on the ground, as no written records suggesting when and why it was built have survived. As far as the western Wansdyke goes, the likelihood is that it was built to mark the boundary between Anglo Saxon settlers and the Romano-British, who were being driven ever further west. One possibility is that it was built, after the Anglo Saxon victory over the British at the Battle of Dyrham in 577, to mark the boundary between the British kingdom of Dumnonia, to the west, and that of the Hwicce. As for who built it, the jury is out. Even if the western Wansdyke was a stand-alone development, unconnected to the eastern Wansdyke, it was a major undertaking, unlikely to have been thrown up hastily in the face of an advancing army. It would have required planning, substantial reserves of manpower and time to carry it to fruition. Ramparts or walls such as this tend to be built by conquering or invading forces, rather than by the people they have displaced. The Wansdyke, however, seems to be an exception to this rule, as the ditch is on the north side of the rampart, making it more difficult to scale from that side. This suggests that it was built by the Romano-British to establish a border, or fallback position, which they hoped would prevail in the event of a Saxon advance.

One thing seems clear: Englishcombe's location behind the border line would have given it strategic importance as a frontier or command post. And perhaps the Norman castle at Englishcombe was built on the site of an earlier stronghold. Indeed, the Rev John Collinson tells us that, 'according to tradition, Inglishcombe was the seat of some of the Saxon kings'. More recently, in their 1923 book on *Somerset*, GW & JH Wade described Englishcombe as 'a small and rather uncouth looking village [which] still retains something of the aloofness which once characterised it as an English outpost of the Welsh border'. Four years later, in *Unknown Somerset*, Donald Maxwell 'found on examining such records as I could obtain of English Combe that Saxon kings had their residence there. Thus the name English was natural in a land ... that looked out upon a Celtic people.' This derivation of Englishcombe's name seems not only attractive but logical, although etymologists tell us that it is just as likely to have started off as Ingwald's combe before being garbled into its current version.

The mysteries of Englishcombe and the Wansdyke seem as far from being solved as ever. But, as much a haven of ancient peace as it may appear today, this assuredly is a place that has lived through turbulent times.

A late 19th-century map of Englishcombe showing the site of Culverhay Castle and the course of the Wansdyke

The official route of the public footpath lies through the KG opposite, before joining Washpool Lane further down, but the official route seems to be little used and you may find it blocked by vegetation. As the lane carries on downhill, it comes to a ford across the Padley Brook, beside which is a footbridge.[1] *Carry on as it leads up the other side of the valley, and, when you come to a row of cottages on the left, you can look through a gate on the right to see the site of Culverhay Castle.*

In 1086, the Domesday Book recorded that 'Inglis-combe' was held by Nigel de Gournay, who had come over with the Conqueror. A culver was a dove and a hay was an enclosure, which implies that Culverhay had an enclosure with a dovecote. In the late 12th century a deer park was established here, and in the mid-13th century the original wooden castle was probably rebuilt in stone. The castle's most notorious resident was Sir Thomas de Gournay. Indicted for his part in the murder of Edward II at Berkeley Castle, he fled abroad, but was captured. Despite orders from Edward III to bring him back alive, he died in mysterious circumstances on the voyage home. Englishcombe, along with the rest of his estates, was confiscated by the crown, and passed to the Duchy of Cornwall, which still owns it today. Whether the castle was abandoned at this time is not clear; Collinson, writing in 1791, said that the building 'had been demolished near a couple of centuries'.[2]

When you come to a T junction, turn right, passing English-combe's old smithy on the right. *After 75m, as the lane bears left uphill, turn right by a triangular patch of grass.* Yeoman's Cottage, which you pass on the right, is believed to have been a beerhouse in the 19th century. *After passing the old vicarage on the left, turn right down a lane, following it as it swings left before climbing steps on the left into the churchyard*, which stands, like the castle, on an eminence. If you bear right towards the edge of the churchyard and look through a gap in the trees, you will see one of the most impressive sections of the western Wansdyke.

Head past the church, probably built by Robert de Gournay in the 12th century, *and go through a gate.* As you head on up the lane you cross the course of the Wansdyke, all trace of which has been obliterated at this point. Just beyond 17th-century Rectory Farm is a tithe barn built by the Prior of Bath Abbey in the early 14th century – possibly with stone from the castle – and restored in the 1990s.[3]

1 On Thorpe's map of 1742, the Padley Brook is identified as the Ingle Brook, but this name has long fallen into disuse.
2 For more on Englishcombe, see Manco, *The Parish of Englishcombe* (www.englishcombe. net/pdf/englishcombe history - manco.pdf)
3 The claim that the barn was built 'out of the ruins of the castle' was made by Tunstall (1848), p.207.

Above: Englishcombe church

Below: The tithe barn c1910

Bottom: Heading west from Englishcombe

Turn right by Rectory Farm, carrying straight on when the road forks. After Manor Farm, the tarmac ends and you continue westward along a green lane. This drops down a dark and rocky way, running with water, to a causeway across a brook, before climbing to resume its level, tree-shaded course. (Ignore a footpath branching right at the top of the rise.)

The return of tarmac signals your entry to Inglesbatch, past more Duchy prop-

erties (batch being a local word for a tump or hill). **Bear right at a T junction by Corner Cottage (but don't turn right again beside it). After passing a large Wesleyan Methodist chapel, now converted to a house called the Chantry, fork right by a phone box. At the farm gates, follow the lane to the right** (ST702613). **The tarmac soon peters out, and, when the lane ends at a gate, turn left to follow a narrow path. After dropping down to a ford with stepping stones, the path climbs to emerge in a field.**

As you **head towards the buildings of Priston Mill, on the far side of the field**, you are around 50m above sea level, compared with 141m on the top of Twerton Round Hill, which is now out of sight beyond the horizon to the right. If you look to your left, though, you will see two more round hills. The hill on the left, with two trees on the top, is Farmborough Common, while the one on the right is Priest Barrow.[1] Although they are now acknowledged to be natural features, there has, over the years, been speculation that they were, like Twerton Round Hill, at least partially man-made. The name Priest Barrow clearly indicates such a belief. Given that

Priston Mill

one of Europe's greatest megalithic sites, at Stanton Drew, is only five miles to the west, such speculation is hardly to be wondered at – and, if nothing else, it adds to the air of brooding mystery this countryside seems to hold.

Priston Mill lies on the other side of the Conygre Brook, which you have to cross on stepping stones – or, to be more precise, a meagre assortment of wobbly rocks. Priston Mill dates back at least to AD931, when it be-

---

1 Farmborough Common is, for obvious reasons, sometimes referred to as Two Tree Hill. However, the trees are so close together that from some angles (as you will see later in the walk) they appear as a single tree. As a result, in some parts the common is known, somewhat confusingly, as One Tree Hill.

longed to Bath Abbey, although the present building dates from the early 18th century. The route you have just followed from Inglesbatch follows the course of an old byway, known as Mill Lane, which fell into disuse in the 20th century. The Hopwood family, who moved into the mill over 40 years ago, revived the business of grinding corn in the traditional way, and for a time the fame of Priston Mill Flour spread far and wide, but, although the machinery still functions, the mill is now a wedding venue.

Head up past the mill, turn left past the tithe barn and continue along a lane. After 200m, turn left along another lane (ST692614). *After 750m, when you come to a T junction, turn left and left again into the village of Priston.*

Priston – originally known as Priest Town, possibly because Priest Barrow lies in the parish – is a delight. In the 1780s, Edmund Rack described it as 'a small village consisting of about 40 houses, most of which are thatched stone cottages, pleasantly situated on a rising ground in a woody vale'. He added that there are 'neither antiquities, manufactures or gentlemen's seats in this parish'. Although thatch has given way to tile, and modern houses have sprung up among the old cottages, much of his description still holds true today.

On the far side of the green stands the village hall – originally a poorhouse, before being converted to a school – with the resolutely unspoilt Ring O'Bells 🍺 beside it.[1] Stepping inside, you are left in little doubt that this is the hub of the community, and not a mere foodie destination for outsiders – although that is not to say the food is not well worth stopping for. In an age when villages are increasingly becoming mere collections of houses, many of whose inhabitants are strangers to each other, it is obvious from even a fleeting visit that Priston has bucked the trend. The highlight of the year is a community festival held over a weekend every September, with the main stage by the village green, and most events free. Although in its current incarnation it only dates back to 2008, it keeps alive the tradition of an annual revel, which in the 18th century, according to Edmund Rack, was held on the Sunday preceding midsummer day.

After a near-obligatory break in the Ring O'Bells, it is worth making a short detour down the road to the left of the pub to visit the church, looking out for a granary raised in the traditional way on staddle stones to keep vermin away from the corn. Above the entrance to the church is a splenetic inscription – 'PRISTON REPENT AND BELEVE THE GOSPEL' – placed there in memory of 'Thomas Wats, Preacher of the Word Of God', whose preaching days came to an end in

1 The Ring O'Bells is open at lunchtimes from Friday to Sunday.

1589. The mighty wooden door leading into the church is believed to date from Norman times, making it one of the oldest in the country.

Perhaps the most striking thing about Priston church, though, is the unfeasibly large weathercock. It was installed on the tower in 1813, a gift of the lord of the manor, who, so legend has it, told the company making it that it was to grace one of the tallest towers in the county. Legend also has it that, before it was hauled up into position, it was filled with beer, which the villagers were invited to imbibe. As the cock is five feet high and six feet long, that must have been some party. Thomas Wats would almost certainly not have approved.

The tower of Priston church, with its unfeasibly large weathercock

Heading back to the Ring O'Bells, bear right to carry on along the road through the village. After 75m, you come to a junction. The building on the opposite corner was another pub, called the Dog, which called last orders in 1966. ***Turn right to follow a lane, past the old smithy, out of the village. After 300m, when the lane forks, bear left*** (ST693602).

Between Priston and Tunley

After a few metres, when the lane bears right up to a house, carry straight on along a footpath beside a stream. Go through a KG and carry on, keeping to the right-hand side of the hedge ahead. At the top of the field bear right along a rough track. A distant row of poplars lends a touch of Gallic insousiance to the scene – and from this angle you can also see why Farmborough Common is sometimes known as One Tree Hill. *Bear left, following a farm track through a gateway. At the end of the field you come to a crosspath known as Blind Lane. Turn right along it* under a vault of trees before emerging into the open with far-reaching views ahead.

As you carry on along the lane, you will see the batch or spoil heap of Priston Colliery ahead – a man-made feature dating back less than a century. Priston – which was actually in the village of Tunley – was the last deep mine opened in Somerset. The first sod was cut in March 1914, and the first coal was brought to the surface just over a year later. Unlike earlier collieries, no railway or

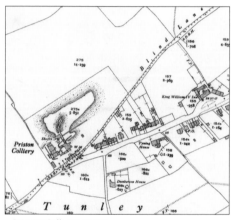

Priston Colliery c1920

Heading down Stoneage Lane to the valley of the Cam Brook

Dunkerton Colliery Halt after closure

tramway was built to serve it, as all coal was carried away by road. It failed to live up to the hopes of its promoters, was sold to new owners in 1923 and closed in 1930.[1] The house on your right, when you reach the main road, was once the colliery office.

Turn left along the main road for 50m, before turning right down Stoneage Lane (ST693594). After passing Lower Tunley Farm, the lane heads down to the valley of the Cam Brook, with a glorious view, over to Carlingcott and the outskirts of Peasedown, more characteristic of upland Derbyshire than Somerset. You are now dropping down to one of the main centres of the Somerset Coalfield; few coalfields were set in such idyllic surroundings.

After swinging right past Bridge Farm, the lane curves left across a bridge over the old Camerton & Limpley Stoke Railway (ST695585). Dunkerton Colliery Halt stood directly below the bridge on the right. Before the railway was built, an earlier bridge crossed the Somersetshire Coal Canal here. *A little further on, you come to Stoneage Cottage, with Gothic-style windows, on the left.*

● *There is an optional diversion here, a there-and-back walk through a glorious meadow to see one of the strangest landscapes in a walk not short of strange landscapes. If you decide to give the diversion a miss, carry on along the lane and skip the next paragraph.*

1 For more information on Priston, Camerton New and Dunkerton Collieries, see Down & Warrington, *The History of the Somerset Coalfield*

● *For the diversion, go through a gate on the right, opposite Stoneage Cottage, and carry on through a meadow. After 500m, go through a KG and turn right. After passing a house, when the path bears left, you will see some cottages ahead with a tree-clad hill to the right of them.* The cottages stood below the bank of the Coal Canal which ran behind them, while the man-made hill is the batch or spoil heap of Camerton New Colliery, which closed as recently as 1950. After the canal fell into disuse, the railway that replaced it did not follow its course along the contours but crossed the field to your left. Today, little trace of either survives. *From here, retrace your steps to Stoneage Cottage and turn right.*

The tree-covered batch of Camerton New Colliery is seen here on the left. The Coal Canal ran behind the cottage on the right, but the railway that replaced it ran to the left of the batch.

● *After 40m, just past Cam Barn, turn left through a gate along a bridleway, which after 200m crosses a bridge over the Cam Brook.* It once continued along the left-hand side of the Cam Brook, but was rerouted across the bridge when Dunkerton Colliery opened in 1905. As you carry on along the right-hand side of the brook, you can see the colliery spoil heap towering above you. Dunkerton Colliery, although only operational for 20 years, was for a time the most productive in the Somerset Coalfield, and the reason why the railway was built to replace the canal. Although tranquillity has now returned to the valley, it is difficult to imagine what it must have been like in the colliery's brief heyday.

When you come to a lane, turn left, passing Splott Farm on the right. The bridge that takes you back across the Cam Brook featured in

DUNKERTON COLLIERY

Dunkerton Colliery had a working life of only 20 years, but during that time it acquired the distinction not only of being the largest colliery in Somerset but also the one with the worst reputation. The contract for sinking the first shaft was signed on 11 May 1903; the first coal was brought to the surface two years later. The company's policy was to extract coal as quickly and as cheaply as possible. Corners were cut, with scant regard to safety, and accidents were common; seams which proved hard to work were abandoned in favour of seams where coal was plentiful. The mine owners had little interest in its long-term viability; they wanted to make the maximum amount of money in the minimum amount of time. Conflict with the workforce was inevitable and it was not long in coming.

By April 1907, there were around 200 carting boys employed at Dunkerton, dragging coal out of the mine by means of that notorious device, the guss and crook. This consisted of a tarred rope which the carting boy wore round his waist; to this was attached a chain, at the other end of which was the crook. This was hooked onto a putt – a sledge filled with coal – which the carting boy would then drag up out of the mine, crawling along on all fours, with the chain between his legs. New boys would find their waists rubbed raw; they were advised to rub their own urine into the sores to toughen up the skin. They received a penny a ton for the first 50 yards covered and a halfpenny for every 50 yards after that. They complained that the roads were rougher at Dunkerton than at other collieries and the putts heavier, and put in for a pay rise, asking for a penny for every 50 yards covered. The company dismissed the claim. The dispute rumbled on for eighteen months until, on 29 October 1908, they came out on strike. Four hundred men came out in support, leaving only about 50 at work, who, because there were no boys to carry the coal, were assigned to exploratory and maintenance duties.

Strike pay from the union was ten shillings a week for the men and five shillings for the boys. Men with families received an additional shilling for each child. There was, inevitably, widespread hardship and, as the striking miners shivered and froze through the long months of a Somerset winter, feeling against those who had stayed at work intensified. On 22 January 1909, with the strike almost three months old, resentment flared into open conflict. As darkness fell, between 150 and 200 strikers gathered at the colliery and set off for Carlingcott singing 'The Dunkerton Carting Boys Song', which had been written for the occasion.

As they approached the colliery manager's house, shots were fired from within and several men fell to the ground. The police intervened to prevent an attack on the house, while the injured men were carried to nearby houses and doctors were summoned. Three men were subsequently transferred to hospital in Bath. The colliery manager's son, who had fired the shots, was charged with unlawful and malicious wounding, but was found not guilty. Fifteen of those who had taken part in the demonstration, however, despite no evidence of actual violence being proved against them, were sentenced to periods of imprisonment with hard labour.

The strike ended on 18 February, when the men and boys returned to work pending arbitration. However, a court appointed by the Board of Trade decided that the carting boys' rates of pay were fair and should not be increased. Although relations between management and workforce failed to improve, and the colliery's reputation as a hellish place to work deepened, productivity soared. By the 1920s, however, thanks to the cavalier attitude of the owners, time was running out for Dunkerton Colliery and it was decided to close it in May 1925. It was kept ticking over for a couple of years, in case anyone wanted to take it on, but it finally closed in September 1927. Despite numerous proposals to reopen it, including one by the newly-formed National Coal Board in 1946, that was the end of one of Somerset's grimmest pits.

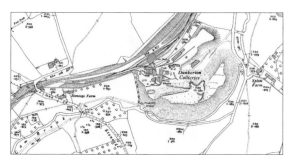

The Titfield Thunderbolt, with the squire, John Gregson, driving over it shortly before finding the road blocked by Sid James's steamroller. A little further on, you pass gates guarding the entrance to the old colliery – now home to Dunkerton Dismantlers. It was in the colliery sidings – since obliterated by tipping – that the duel between the Titfield Thunderbolt and the aforementioned steamroller took place. As you carry on, you can see a line of trees marking the course of the old railway ahead. ***After passing sewage works, turn right at a junction to continue along the valley*** (ST701590), looking out for the tower of Dunkerton church through the trees.

Dunkerton village 1891

When you reach Dunkerton village, you may wish to cross the brook for a closer look at the church and the old buildings surrounding it. To carry on, however, ***turn left up a lane called The Hollow.*** Just past the village hall, you will see Viaduct Cottage on the left. Its name recalls a five-arched railway viaduct, demolished by explosives in 1981, that crossed high above the road. A little further up the lane, after passing Crooked Cottage – with a datestone of 1695 – you will see a parking area cut into the bank on the left. Just past it, the canal, curving to the north of the route later taken by the railway, crossed the road on an aqueduct which was demolished in the 1960s.

Carry on past Manor Farm as the lane grows ever steeper and narrower, before curving up to the main Tunley road. Cross and turn right for a few metres to where a footpath sign points left. Before following it, look a little way along the road to see a lost pub – the

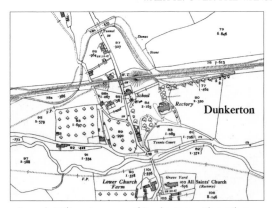

An early 20th-century map of Dunkerton, with a railway viaduct and a disused canal aqueduct crossing The Hollow. Both have long since been demolished.

John Bull Inn – on the other side of the road. *Carry on through a handgate to follow a path along the edge of a field with the hedge on your right.* As you *head into the next field,* the views open up ahead, with that line of poplars – now more distant – over to the left.

To your right is Duncorn Hill, 178m above sea level, upon which, according to Collinson, 'once stood a Carnedd, or pile of stones, erected by our British forefathers to notify some victory, or other memorable event, to succeeding ages.' Collinson also claimed that the name of Dunkerton, 'being compounded of Dun, a hill, Carn, a monument of stones, and Ton, a town, signifies the town near the Carnedd mountain'.

At the end, go through a handgate (ST707607) *and follow a path past old houses.* This is the hamlet of Nailwell, and the building by the crossroads at the end is another long-lost pub called the Malt & Hops.

Near Kilkenny Cottages

187

The Padley valley and Barrow Castle

Turn right, carry straight on at the crossroads, but, 100m further on, when a lane branches right, turn along it. This is Kilkenny Lane, a name which may date from Saxon times, for in AD925 Robert le Bok was acquitted of arson after a house belonging to John de Kylkenny in Chelwood, two miles west of Farmborough, burnt down. Over to your left, in the distance, you can see the upper terraces of Bath, including Lansdown Crescent. Although far from being the most spectacular distant view of the city, this is in many ways the strangest, underlining the sheer improbability of such a dazzling showpiece of a city being set down amidst this unassuming countryside.

After 1100m, with wide rolling fields on either side, you will see some buildings – Kilkenny Cottages – at the edge of the woods ahead. Just before them, cross a rickety stile on the left and carry on with the hedge on your right (ST723615). *At the end of the field, cross a stile, head on through a KG, but, instead of carrying on alongside the hedge, head straight ahead downhill across the field.*

When you come to where the hedgerow juts out at an obtuse angle, bear right to follow a well-defined track downhill, heading in the direction of the large modern school building in the distance. The battlemented building to the right of it is Barrow Castle, built in the late 1850s by the Rev Riley, a clergyman from Bristol. Although it would have been a good site for one, there is no record of an earlier castle here; its name derives from nearby Barrow Hill – otherwise known as Twerton Round Hill. Thorpe's map of 1742, however, shows a Barrow House in roughly the same location, and it is possible that Barrow Castle was a rebuilding of this.

Go through a KG and carry on down the valley. Partway down the field, you will see a gate leading into the woods on your left. Don't go through it, but look to your right to see the faint outline of a ramparted ditch silhouetted against the sky (ST726623). Although far less impressive than the section you saw at Englishcombe, this is the Wansdyke.

Cross a footbridge over the Padley Brook, go through a KG and follow a path up a slope whose steepness suggests it could have formed part of a defensive fortification. *Steps have been provided to make the climb easier; when the path forks, follow these up to the right and carry on between fences. Go through a KG, carry on along a lane and, at the main road, cross and turn right up Rush Hill. After 350m, turn left along Somerdale View, and right up a path at the end. At the top, carry on along a road leading away from the escarpment, and at the second crossroads, turn left along Bloomfield Drive.*

After 150m, you pass a bus stop, where you can, if you wish, catch a bus back to the city centre.

Otherwise, carry on, and, after another 200m, as you approach the main road, you will see a high wall, looking almost like a relic of some old fortification, with Bath's highest and least-known crescent – Bloomfield Crescent, built in the 1790s – behind it. *After turning left at the end,* the back of the crescent can be seen through a gateway; the front, with a panoramic view across Bath, has no public access.

Carry on downhill, passing the entrance to the Tumps, one of Bath's lesser-known open spaces, on the right. Further down, you come to Westfield Lodge, guarding the entrance to Westfield House. After crossing the end of Englishcombe Lane, you pass Bloomfield House, with the blank windows in its end wall painted in trompe l'oeil style.

When you come to Wellsway, carry on along it, crossing to the right-hand side at the pedestrian lights. When Wellsway bears left, carry on, before forking left to head down Holloway, the old way into the city from the south. At the bottom, carry on along the road as it levels out, and, at the end, carry on along a footpath past St Mark's church. Continue along St Mark's Road, turn left down Lyncombe Hill and right at the bottom, before crossing at the pedestrian lights. Cross the footbridge over the river, go through the tunnel under the railway and carry on along Manvers Street to return to the starting point.

The Legend of Twerton Round Hill

As long ago as the 14th century, the official name of the 141m-high round hill that overlooks Twerton was High Barrow. It was also known as Englishcombe Barrow, High Barrow Hill, Round Barrow or simply Barrow Hill. It has been known colloquially as Twerton Round Hill, however, for well over 200 years – the first reference to it as such appeared in the *Bath Chronicle* on 6 November 1794. By the time Twerton Parish Council acquired it as a public open space in 1907, the name had stuck.

Despite its Silbury-like profile, today there is general agreement that the hill was formed naturally. A council website on green spaces within Bath states that 'the conical shape of Twerton Roundhill was formed as the soft clays that once surrounded it eroded away, leaving a peak of Great Oolite rock or Bath stone.' We only have to go back just over a century, however, to detect a note of uncertainty. MJB Baddeley, in his *Guide to Bath and Bristol and Forty Miles Around*, published in 1902, wrote that Twerton Round Hill 'bears a pronouncedly artificial appearance, but is believed to be natural.'

For the Rev John Collinson, writing in 1791, there was no question but that the hill was man-made, at least in part. He described it as

one of the largest, and most remarkable *barrows* or *tumuli* in the world, which seems to have been intended as a monumental *speculum* for all the adjacent country. This eminence which has been called for ages *Round-Barrow* and *Barrow-Hill*, although it has generally been considered a natural mount, stands on the brow of a high ridge of hills, about half a mile eastward from the village of Inglishcombe ... Conjecture itself cannot rest satisfied concerning the origin of this immense mount; it might have been raised in commemoration of some signal victory, or it might to this day cover the reliques and spoils of some great warrior.

John Wood, writing around 50 years earlier, suggested another candidate:

There are people who tell us, that it was a sepulchral monument, raised in honour of some great person; while others, who imagine it above the power of human art or industry to raise so large a hill, and yet believe it raised, ascribe it to the devil, and say, that as he was going by that place with a wheelbarrowful of rubbish, taken up by him upon Odd Down, he grew weary with his load, and discharging it there

Opposite: The western flank of Twerton Round Hill

made the round mount that now appears; which, as it consisted but of one barrowful of rubbish, was therefore, say they, called Barrow Hill. This remarkable mount seems to me to have been King Bladud's sepulchre.

As late as 1848, James Tunstall wrote confidently in his book of *Rambles about Bath*, that it was

the largest and most remarkable burial ground in the world. At its base it is 800 yards in circumference; its summit is 36 yards in diameter; its eastward slope is 104 yards; its perpendicular height 100 feet. Conjecture has vainly sought for the origin of this immense artificial mound. That it is so, all antiquaries agree, for its form and aspect differ materially from a natural hill.

When REM Peach published a revised edition of

BLADUD, to whom the GRECIANS gave the Name of ABARIS.

Bladud, the legendary founder of Bath, as he appeared in John Wood's *Essay towards a Description of Bath*

Tunstall's work around 40 years later, however, he was just as confi-dent in refuting the idea that the hill was manmade:

Englishcombe Barrow, otherwise Barrow Hill, has, until lately, had the reputation of being an immense artificial mound, and one of the largest barrows in England ... From its peculiar contour, the conjecture, as mentioned by Collinson and others, that it was artificial, was not to be surprised at; but on a visit to the spot by the Somersetshire Archaeological and Natural History Society, in 1876, it was pointed out by Mr Moore that there were undisturbed horizontal beds of oolite on the top, and that originally it had been a continuation of the table land of Odd Down, the separation having been effected by subsequent denudation and that, consequently, the mound was natural and not artificial.

Today, encircled by roads and houses, with its origins now accepted to be purely geological, it is hardly surprising that Twerton Round Hill's mythic status has been forgotten. Standing on the hill, though, and looking westward, or seeing it from a distance silhouetted against the sky, it is still possible to recapture the feeling of awe and wonder it once inspired. And, as a measure of the importance once accorded to it, we only have to recall Great Pulteney Street's alignment with it, which featured at the end of the first walk.

Perhaps the last word, though, should go to a Mr Woodward, who wrote to the *Bath Chronicle* on 14 October 1933, giving a possible reason for the legends surrounding Twerton Round Hill having been forgotten:

> I notice that the height of it is stated to be 467 feet above sea level, but since I first saw it the height appears to me to be less and the top not such a peak as it was. I have noticed for years the surface of the hill with cracks in it several inches wide and of some depth, especially in dry weather. I think it may mean a subsidence, or shrinking of the subsoil. I wonder if anyone else has noticed the apparent lessening of the height of it. I only know of one person beside myself who thinks so, and he estimates the hill to have shrunk by at least 20 feet.

An OS map from 1902 gives the height of Twerton Round Hill as 467 feet above sea level, but if we turn to an OS map from 1958 we find it has dwindled to 463 feet – far less than the 20-foot shrinkage claimed by Mr Woodward, but curious none the less. And as for the change in the hill's profile and what he suspected to be subsidence, does this perhaps give some credence to the legend of the hill having been raised, at least in part, by human rather than natural forces?

Into the East: Walk 13
Farleigh Down, Box Hill & Corsham

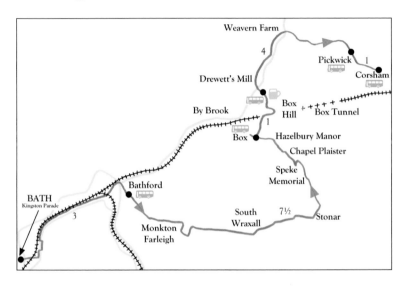

Distance: 16½ miles; ends at Corsham, from where there is a regular
bus service (X31) back to Bath
shorter options available by:
catching a bus (3) to Bathford at the start of the walk;
catching a bus (X31) back to Bath from Box, Box Hill or Pickwick

Terrain: Generally straightforward, although with over 20 stiles and
some muddy sections; sheep and cattle are likely to be encountered
at various points

Pubs and cafés:
Quarrymans Arms, Box Hill; lunch served 12-3 Mon-Fri, food
served all day Sat & Sun (www.quarrymans-arms.co.uk; 01225
743569)

Map: OS Explorer 155 & 156; or AA Walker's Map 25 & OS
Explorer 156

Opposite: Heading east into Wiltshire across Farleigh Down

This walk, unlike the previous ones, is not circular, but ends at Corsham, from where there are regular buses back to Bath. It starts by heading east along the Kennet & Avon Canal, before crossing the river and climbing to the breezy heights of Farleigh Down. From there we cross the high ground eastward to Monkton Farleigh, past a medieval conduit which once supplied water to a Cluniac priory. After exploring the village, we follow a stately avenue of trees to South Wraxall, whose manor house dates from the 15th century, and Stonar, whose school occupies a mansion designed by two of Bath's most prolific 18th-century architects.

From there, we head north, across a lost and lonely plateau, a land of tiny hamlets, dry-stone walls, little-walked footpaths, overgrown stiles and tracks through fields of barley. En route, we cross the Roman road from Bath to London (once thought to have formed part of the Wansdyke), see the spot where a famous explorer met an untimely end and visit a medieval pilgrim's chapel which, in the 18th century, became the lair of a notorious highwayman. After following a tree-lined drive to Hazelbury Manor, we skirt the high ground above the village of Box, past ancient quarries and the spoil heaps above Box Tunnel, before calling into an alehouse once frequented by quarrymen.

Leaving the high ground, we drop down to the valley of the By Brook, which we follow past old mills and farmhouses, before climbing through ancient woodland and following quiet lanes to the historic weaving town of Corsham.

From Kingston Parade, head east along York Street. Turn right at the end and bear left by the Huntsman pub along North Parade. Cross at the lights, carry on along North Parade and cross at the lights at the end of North Parade Road. Bear left for a few metres before turning through an archway under the railway bridge. Follow a path up steps to the canal and turn left along the towpath.

When you come to a road bridge, climb a flight of steps, turn right and cross a zebra crossing before continuing along the right bank of the canal. After 300m, follow the towpath as it crosses the canal at the back of the former canal company offices and go through a tunnel to emerge in a cutting through Sydney Gardens. After going through another tunnel, carry on along the towpath for 2000m, and, after going under Bridge 183, just past the George Inn, head over to the lane on the left and carry on in the same direction. After crossing a stile at the end of the lane (ST782666), *cross the railway line with care, head down steps, go through a kissing gate (KG) and follow a track across a large field. Go through another KG, follow a path up the railway embankment and carry on across the bridge.*

When you reach the road, cross and turn right, following the pavement across a footbridge. Cross the road and go up Ostlings Lane to the right of the Crown Inn.

If travelling by bus from Bath, get off just past the Crown Inn, cross the road and go up Ostlings Lane to the right of the Crown.

At the top of Ostlings Lane, go up a path to the left of the church lych-gate. Continue up Mountain Wood Road, but, when it bears left, carry on up the grass. After 75m, cross a stile on the right (ST790665) *and head diagonally uphill across a field.*

Cross another stile and carry on up through the woods in the same direction. At a crosspath, turn right for a few metres, before turning left and carrying on uphill. At the next crosspath, bear right and then left up a stepped path. When it forks, bear right. At the top, carry straight on along a footpath between two low, moss-covered stone walls which leads from Somerset into Wiltshire.

Go through a gate (ST795658) *and carry on along a strip of greensward.* Deep underground lies a labyrinth of underground quarries, covering over 100 acres. After quarrying ended in the 1930s, the tunnels were acquired by the War Office for use as a vast underground ammunition dump. *When you reach the trees at the far end, bear right past a small farm building. After crossing a lane, head straight on through a field with a hedge on your right, and a view southwards to the White Horse at Westbury.*

Climbing to Farleigh Down

Cross a stile and carry on past industrial buildings on the site of Sheep Drove Quarry, where a vertical shaft dropped down to galleries far below. *At the end of the track, cross a stile onto a lane, and carry straight on across another stile to follow a path* past a conduit which supplied water to a nearby Cluniac priory. It was built in the 14th century, but its roof dates from a restoration in 1784.

After crossing a stile at the end of the path (ST805657), *carry on past Home Farm. When you reach a lane, bear right along it. After 250m, when you come to a T junction, bear left past a lodge with an ornamental chimney. Carry on through the village of Monkton Farleigh*, passing old stone cottages and a house with a shell porch and a 1736 datestone. The church, a little further on, has a 12th-century doorway and a 13th-century tower, although the rest of it was rebuilt in 1844.

The conduit at Monkton Farleigh

The tree-lined avenue leading eastwards from the manor house

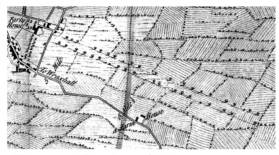

The avenue on Thorpe's map of 1742

After another 100m, turn left, following a signpost to Kingsdown. After *300m*, when you come to a bench beside the road, look to the left to see the early Georgian manor house, which includes fragments of the Cluniac priory, founded in 1125. A few metres further on, ***cross a stile on the right and head along the tree-lined avenue leading away from the manor.***

After 1100m, cross a stile and carry on. At the end of the avenue, cross another stile to the right of the gateposts. Cross a lane, go through a gateway and head across a field to a stile. Carry on along a narrow path, cross another pair of stiles, head over to a KG and turn right along a lane (ST831654).

South Wraxall Manor in 1887

The drive branching off through the gates a few metres along on the left is the original course of the road, which ran past South Wraxall Manor. When the current road was built, the old one was downgraded to a footpath, which the owner of the manor closed off over 15 years ago. Now, the only glimpse you get of the manor is through another gate 150m further on. The manor, which dates from the 15th century, was described by John Aubrey in the 17th century as 'a very large well built old house'.

According to legend, it was also the first place Sir Walter Raleigh smoked tobacco in England. Since 2006, it has been the home of John Taylor of Duran Duran and his wife Gela Nash-Taylor, founder of Juicy Couture. A little further along is Manor Farm, largely hidden from view, which is thought to have been built in the 14th century as a hospice and chapel dedicated to St Audoen.

At the main road, cross and go through a gate which may be reluctant to open. Carry on beside a hedge, cross a stile at the end and go through a gate to the right of the pylon ahead (ST843658). *A little further on, turn right along a farm track. After going through another gate, you come to Stonar School*, which was founded in 1895 at Sandwich in Kent, but moved here in 1939. It took over a building known as Cottle's House, built by John Palmer and Thomas Jelly of Bath around 1778, whose west-facing castellated bays can be seen behind the outbuildings that have sprung up around it.

When the drive swings right, follow a track straight on through a gateway (ST850656) *and turn left. After going through two squeeze stiles, follow a faint track across a field. Go through another squeeze stile and carry on alongside the hedge on your left. At the end of the field, negotiate an overgrown track in the corner and cross a stile* (ST850662). *Carry on for a few metres before bearing right alongside a ditch and carrying straight on through another field. Cross a stile by a metal gate and carry on with Cottles Wood on your right. At the end of the field, you cross the course of the Roman Road from London to Bath,* once a busy highway before slowly falling into disuse and total dereliction. The abandoned track through a tumbledown wooden gate into private woods on the right follows its course (ST848667). This road was once thought to have formed part of the Wansdyke, and is shown as such on old OS maps, but this theory is now largely discredited (see pages 174-5). *Go through the metal handgate ahead and carry on through a rough field dominated by the gaunt remains of a dead oak.*

At the main road, cross a slab stile on the opposite side of the road a few metres along to the right. Head for a stile in the opposite hedgerow, cross it

The Speke Memorial

and turn left. At the end, cross a lane to continue along a rough track between the cottages of Lower Wadswick (ST846673).

Carry on across a field, heading towards another group of cottages, and turn left along a lane. After 100m, just past Chapel Cottage – once used by the Plymouth Brethren – *turn left, following a permissive waymark up steps by a parking area, go through a handgate with a bell and head across a field.*

After 150m, cross a slab stile ahead. Before carrying on, divert left for 250m to find a memorial to the African explorer John Hanning Speke, who died here 'by the accidental explosion of his gun' on 15 September 1864 (ST843674).[1]

Retrace your steps and carry on alongside a fence, before crossing two stiles to emerge on a lane (ST840678). *Turn left and cross the main road with care.* The building opposite, now known as Bell House, was once the Bell Inn. At the far end is a medieval chapel known as Chapel Plaister. In 1536, John Leland described it as a hermitage, but according to John Aubrey, writing over a century later, it 'was heretofore a place of entertainment for Pilgrims that went to Glastonbury'.

An early 20ᵗʰ-century postcard of Chapel Plaister

In the 18ᵗʰ century, it became the hideout of a highwayman called John Poulter, alias Baxter. He was apprehended in 1753 after stealing a watch from a Dr Hancock of Salisbury as he rode across Claverton

---

1 For information on the circumstances of and controversy surrounding Speke's death, see Elliott, *Foul Deeds & Suspicious Deaths in Bath.*

Down. In an attempt to escape hanging, he not only turned King's Evidence but wrote a book, *The Discoveries of John Poulter*, naming and shaming his former accomplices and telling readers how they could guard themselves against such ne'er-do-wells. It became a runaway bestseller, but Poulter did not live to reap the rewards of his literary success. After languishing in Ilchester Gaol for almost a year, and despite a daring but short-lived bid for freedom, he was hanged in March 1754.

The chapel was later occupied as a cottage, but by the early 19th century had become a wood store. By the time James Tunstall visited in the 1840s, it was in a sad state. 'Its altar,' he lamented, 'is now an oven, bean stalks occupy its chancel, and fowls roost in the loft.' In 1894, however, after the curate of Box launched a fundraising campaign, it was finally restored as a place of worship. Another restoration was carried out in 1999 and the building is usually open between 2 and 4pm on Wednesdays in the summer.

Bear left along the verge for a few metres, turn right across the grass and go through a handgate beside the gates of Hazelbury Manor. As you walk along the drive, the manor, parts of which date from the 14th century, appears ahead. ***After passing the gateposts at the end, turn left, carry on along a track (ignoring a bridleway branching left) and go through a squeeze stile beside a gate.*** As you follow a track between fences, you pass an artificial mound on the right, raised in the 1980s in homage to the prehistoric monuments that are so prominent a feature of Wiltshire's landscape. The manor gardens, which are occasionally open to the public, also contain a stone circle constructed around the same time.

Hazelbury Manor

The artificial mound raised in the 1980s

Looking over the village of Box

At the end of the track is a stile (ST831683), *beyond which is a superb view over the village of Box. Here you have the option of cutting the walk short and heading back to Bath or of carrying on.*

To cut the walk short, head down the old packhorse trail ahead which soon becomes a tarmaced road leading into the village of Box, where there is a pub – the Queen's Head – and buses back to Bath.

To carry on, bear right along a path and after 400m, bear left at a T junction (ST833686). *A few metres further on, bear right to follow a path through woods, with a wall on your right and old quarries below you on the left.* In the 17th century, John Aubrey wrote that

> the quarry at Haselbury was most eminent for freestone in the western parts, before the discovery of the Portland quarry, which was but about anno 1600 ... Malmesbury Abbey and the other Wiltshire religious houses are of Haselbury stone. The old tradition is that St Aldhelm, Abbot of Malmesbury, did throw down his glove, and bad them dig there, and they should find great treasure, meaning the quarry.

When you reach a road, turn right along it. The large spoil heap – now an adventure playground – you pass on the right was formed when Box railway tunnel was excavated between 1836 and 1841. Hidden in the woods is a shaft, protected by a high wall, used during the construction of the tunnel and retained for ventilation. *Turn left at the crossroads*, past a creeper-covered building used as an inn by the navvies building the tunnel, *and after 100m turn left along a footpath by Berry Cottage* (ST837692).

Woods above the old quarries at Hazelbury

The former Box Tunnel Inn

After bearing right when the path forks, you will see a garden created in a quarry on your right. Carry on, bearing right past a row of quarrymen's cottages, to the Quarrymans Arms 🍺, *whose walls are adorned with tools once used in nearby quarries* (ST834693).

Head down steps in the far corner of the pub car park and continue down a steep path with superb views. Turn right down a rough track and bear right up a lane, down which a tramway carried stone to a yard beside the railway in the 19th century. *After 120m, just before a junction, bear left across a stone stile.*

🚌 *If you want to make your way back to Bath at this point, don't cross the stile, but turn left a few metres further on, and you will find a westbound bus stop on the left at the end of the lane.*

Having crossed the stile, follow steps down to the main road and cross to an eastbound bus stop which stands on the site of the Rising Sun, destroyed in 1957 by a gas explosion which killed the landlord, along with his wife and four-year-old son. *Cross a*

stile, carry on downhill, and, after crossing another stile, continue down a lane to cross the By Brook at Drewett's Mill. Turn right and, after 120m, cross a stile on the right (ST831700) *to carry on through fields alongside the By Brook for 800m.*

Drewett's Mill c1900

Along the By Brook

The ruins of Weavern Farm

The stone in Hungerford Wood

At a lane, bear right past Widdenham Farm, which was originally a 17th-century mill house. *Continue past turnings to right and left, but, when you come to a gate ahead, turn left. At a rough track, bear right past an impressive barn. Just beyond it, bear right through a gateway following a footpath sign* (ST836711). *Carry on in the same direction for 600m, and after heading downhill, go through a stile into woodland owned by the Woodland Trust* (ST840716).

Carry on down a holloway and, after crossing a bridge, you will see the ruins of Weavern Farm to your left. Another mill, which closed in the 1830s, stood beside it. *Go through a handgate, bear right across a brook and follow a track winding uphill. After going through a handgate into Hungerford Wood, continue past a crosspath a few metres further on. After the track curves right, turn left down a holloway by a large stone with a hole in it* (ST844715). Its original function is unclear: it may simply be a boundary stone, but, in this sequestered and vaguely sinister spot, is it too fanciful to imagine that it was placed here to ward off the power of evil spirits, like similar witch or hag stones elsewhere?.

Just after the track levels out and crosses a brook, follow a foot-path sign across a stile on the right and head steeply uphill. Carry on across a stile, but, when you come to a horse chestnut, turn left along a track (ST850712)*, with Pickwick Lodge over to your right. Cross a stile by a gate and carry on in the same direction. Continue through a gate, following a lane past Hillsgreen Lodge. When you come to the gate of Church Farm, follow the lane right. At the main road, turn right and cross to the Hare & Hounds* (ST863706)*.*

After turning left at the mini-roundabout by the Hare & Hounds, you have a choice.

🚌 *To catch a bus back to Bath, turn right at the next mini-roundabout along Valley Road, where you will find a bus stop a little way along on the right.*

Otherwise, carry on along the road. Modern houses, along with impressive 19th-century villas, predominate for a time before older buildings start to reappear. Look for the former White Lion, still with its sign bracket, on the corner of Paul Road. Alexander Terrace, on the left, holds a surprise in the form of a first-floor bay, with well-proportioned columns, partway along a row of late Victorian cottages.

Carry on along Pickwick Road and, at the mini roundabout, cross at the lights and carry on in the same direction. At the Methuen Arms, with the 18th-century Grove on your right, turn left along the High Street. John Betjeman thought this street 'one of the best left in England', while that doyen of architectural

In Corsham High Street

Corsham's Flemish Weaver pub

Church Street

historians, Nikolaus Pevsner, declared that Corsham had 'no match in Wiltshire for its wealth of good houses'. If it looks familiar, that may be because in 2014 it was transformed into 18th-century Truro for the BBC production of *Poldark*.

As you carry on along the High Street, you come to the Flemish Weaver, once the Packhorse, its renaming recalling the weavers from the Low Countries who settled here in the 17th century. The town hall, next door, was built as a market hall, with open arches, in 1784. After they were filled in, the upper storey was added in 1882.

A right turn along Church Street, past old weavers' cottages, leads to an imposing three-storey mid-18th-century house, beyond which lies Corsham's most bizarre building. You could be forgiven for thinking that the ruin set back behind a wall on the left is part of some ancient monastery – which is probably what you are meant to think. It

The 18th-century folly

The school and almshouses founded in 1668

is actually an 18th-century folly, built so that the owners of Corsham Court did not have to look at the back of that imposing three-storey building. *The entrance to the court, open to the public and long famous for its collection of paintings, is a little further along in Church Square.*

A right turn through a gateway leads along tree-lined South Avenue, with Corsham Park to your left. At the end, go through a KG to see, opposite, a row of almshouses, together with a school and master's house, founded in 1668 to accommodate six elderly people and educate ten scholars. Little changed in three and a half centuries, they are open to the public and provide a unique glimpse into 17th-century life.

Head straight on past the almshouses along Pound Pill and after 200m you will come to a bus stop with regular services back to Bath. 🚌

Into the East: Walk 14
Claverton Down, Avoncliff &
Bradford on Avon

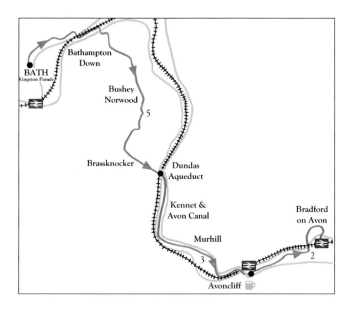

Distance: 10 miles; ends at Bradford on Avon, from where there is a
   regular train service back to Bath
   a shorter option is available by catching a train from Avoncliff to
   Bath

Terrain: Some rough and rocky paths on Claverton Down, and one
   difficult road crossing; otherwise straightforward; sheep and cattle
   are likely to be encountered at various points

Pubs and cafés:
   Cross Guns, Avoncliff; food served all day (www.
   crossgunsavoncliff.com; 01225 862335)

Map: OS Explorer 155, 142 & 156; or AA Walker's Map 25

Opposite: The packhorse bridge at Bradford on Avon

Like the previous walk, this walk ends not in Bath but in one of Wiltshire's historic weaving towns. This time the destination is Bradford on Avon, as hilly as Corsham is flat, and one of the most architecturally fascinating small towns in England.

We start by heading up to Claverton Down and following rocky paths through woods and old quarries which once inspired Gainsborough. After passing the sites of some celebrated foul deeds and some mysterious standing stones, we drop down to the Avon valley to follow one of the most scenic stretches of the Kennet & Avon Canal. After crossing two spectacular aqueducts and visiting a riverside pub, we end with a brief exploration of some of Bradford on Avon's treasures before catching a train back to Bath.

From Kingston Parade, head north round the Abbey and carry on along the High Street. Continue along Northgate Street, bearing to the right of St Michael's church to head along Walcot Street, and carry on along London Street. At Cleveland Place, cross straight ahead over two sets of lights and continue along the right-hand side of the London Road.

After 400m, carry on across the entrance to a supermarket car park, and after another 50m, by a telephone kiosk, bear right to continue along Kensington Place. After passing Nº 10, turn right down an access road, and at the end go through a gap in the fence to the left of metal gates. Bear left and head diagonally across to the far corner of the meadow. Carry on through a gate and, after another 50m, bear right across a bridge. After going under a railway bridge, turn left along a grassy track beside the railway. Follow this track for 550m, crossing a stile partway along, and at the end go through a kissing gate (KG) onto a lane (ST769662)*. Turn right over the canal and continue up the lane. At the top turn left along a road. After 150m, opposite a house called Avonstone, cross and go up a short flight of steps. Faced with a choice of footpaths, bear right through a squeeze stile and follow a path uphill between fences.*

View northward to the caterpillar of trees on Freezing Hill

After going through a KG at the top, cross the main road and head straight up a footpath with a high fence on the right and a spring on the left. The path includes two flights of wooden steps with handrails, the second of which commands a superb view of Little Solsbury, Lansdown and the caterpillar of trees on Freezing Hill.

From here the path leads into woodland – and it is easy to go astray. Aim to carry on uphill, bearing slightly left towards the spring and crossing it on a plank bridge. After going through a KG, bear left uphill, ignoring a waymarked path heading off down to the left.

Bathampton Down

When you emerge onto Bathampton Down, bear left through the remains of bronze or iron age field systems and settlements. Carry on along a well-walked track which eventually turns into a sunken way heading downhill. As it descends, cross a stile on the right to follow a rough path through the woods (ST775655).

After 300m, you come to a path heading steeply downhill, which follows the course of an inclined plane (see page 122). *Cross it to carry on through a quarry, and, when the track forks, bear right, following a Bath Skyline waymark.* Just past it, look up to the right to see a particularly impressive outcrop. This area, riven by centuries of quarrying, was one of Gainsborough's favourite places to sketch when he lived in Bath between 1759 and 1774. Although the scenery is just as remarkable today, do watch your step while admiring its picturesque qualities – there are plenty of trip hazards and several sheer drops.

After 300m, a broad track curving in from the right leads to old

Following a track through old quarries

underground quarries. The largest is sealed off, but to the left of it is a narrow gap through which two boys crawled in search of adventure in September 1893. Sliding back some stones, they found, not the buried treasure they hoped for, but the body of a young woman called Elsie Luke who had disappeared two years earlier. The ensuing inquest aroused enormous interest, but, although it was clear she had been 'cruelly murdered' and a suspect was identified, no one was ever convicted of her murder.[1]

Entrances to underground quarries

A little further on, when the track forks, bear left and go through a KG into Bushey Norwood. Bear right to follow a faint track alongside the southern ramparts of Bathampton Camp. When the track forks, bear left to head south past patches of uneven ground, the legacy of excavations in the 1880s which discovered evidence of an iron age settlement. As

1 For more on the murder of Elsie Luke, see Elliott, *Foul Deeds & Suspicious Deaths in Bath.*

Emerging onto Bushey Norwood

you approach the south-west corner of the field, look over to your left to see a couple of standing stones (ST780644). Similar stones lie round about, giving rise to speculation that a stone circle once stood here. The truth is almost certainly more prosaic, although whether the stones were connected with an 18th-century racecourse that stood nearby or were raised up for some other reason is unclear. More on the myths and speculations that the stones have generated can be found on pages 227-33.

Racing was already under way on ground to the west of Bushey Norwood by 1721, but in 1759, after Ralph Allen acquired the land, he put a stop to it. After his death, it was revived, and by 1770, when a new grandstand and stables were built, Bath Races were among the highlights of the season. On 18 September 1777, the *Bath Chronicle* reported that 'about 800 carriages, and not less than 20,000 persons on horseback and afoot, were on the Down yesterday, when, it was generally allowed, the sport was equal to any ever seen on a racecourse in one day'. In November the following year, the racecourse was the venue for a notorious duel between Count Rice and the Vicomte du Barré, in which Du Barré was killed.[1] The racecourse closed six years later when the current one on Lansdown opened.[2]

Cross a stepped slab stile in the corner of the field and follow a path past the university bobsleigh track. At a T junction, turn left and then right. After passing metal gates, turn left along a road for

1 For more information see Elliott, *Foul Deeds & Suspicious Deaths in Bath*.
2 For more on the racecourse, see Fawcett, *Bath Entertain'd*.

100m, before turning right along a muddy track with a sign warning of its unsuitability for motors. This is Limekiln Lane, with views over the Claverton valley on the left and evidence of quarrying on the right. On the slopes below the lane was once a vineyard where black cluster and muscadine grapes were grown.

When you come to another road, turn right along the pavement. After 175m, just after passing Bramley Cottages, cross and go through a KG into Rainbow Wood Farm. Follow a path through a succession of KGs, and, after 800m, go through a gate, cross the road and turn left. After 40m, turn right through a KG (ST776629)*, and bear left to follow a track diagonally across a field past Wessex Water HQ. Continue through two KGs and, after passing an old quarry, carry on across the busy Brassknocker Hill and cross a slab stile beside a turnpike trust boundary marker.*

Head down a path with the old Brassknocker Inn, closed around 1870, over to your right. Follow the path as it curves right, and, after crossing a patch of boggy ground, go through a KG into a field with a superb view over the Limpley Stoke valley.

As you bear left downhill alongside a fence, you can see the Gothick splendour of Combe Hill House, dating from around 1794, over to your right. After passing a stile with a gap beside it, continue down a steep incline to a KG which issues straight onto the busy A36 Warminster Road (ST783626)*. This crossing needs extreme care, especially if you have dogs or children with you, and if in a group you are advised to cross one at a time. It can only be hoped that measures will be taken to make this busy crossing safer.*

Once across, turn right for a few metres before heading down a stepped footpath at the start of a lay-by. This leads to Dundas Wharf on the Kennet & Avon Canal. Turn right along the towpath, crossing what was once the junction with the Somersetshire Coal Canal, before heading out onto Dundas Aqueduct.

On the far side of the aqueduct, the canal, having now crossed into Wiltshire, curves right along the east side of the Avon valley, passing a lengthman's cottage and the remains of a stop gate. Today, this section of the canal, with a wooded bank on the left and a steep drop on the right, is a delight. Its construction, however, entailed earth moving and excavation on a gargantuan scale, and, when newly built, it would have cut a raw

Dundas Aqueduct

and rocky swathe through this green valley. After 300m, you can look across to where the Midford Brook flows into the Avon. Beyond it, an eleven-arch viaduct, built in 1833-4, carries the Warminster road across the valley. At its northern end is the former Viaduct Inn, built around the same time, but closed in 2005. High above it, you should also be able to make out the Brassknocker Inn, which lost most of its passing trade when the road along the valley opened.

South of the viaduct, the road climbs out of the valley, and the noise of traffic recedes. After passing Bridge 175, and the remains of another stop gate, you can see Limpley Stoke across the valley, with the name of the village clearly visible on the platform of its railway station. Although the line is still open, however, the last train called here in 1966, and the

Between Dundas and Murhill

station, now immaculately restored, is in private hands. Behind it are some impressive buildings, while down by the river a large mill, now home to various companies, is a reminder of the weaving trade that brought such wealth to this valley.

As you carry on, the side of the valley grows

ever steeper, and you can see how engineers had to cut deep into the rock to build the canal. Soon, the station at Freshford, still very much open, comes into view across the river. A little further on, you come to the once bustling community of Murhill Wharf, on the opposite bank of the canal (ST794606). Today, it is as close to a waterside idyll as you are likely to get, but in the early 19th century it would have been noisy, dirty and probably rough as well, for it had a rather dubious beerhouse. In 1846, its landlord, a Mr Ovens, was convicted of receiving stolen goods from ne'er-do-wells who helped themselves to goods from boats plying the canal.[1]

The reason for all this activity was the presence of a large quarry at the top of the hill, from which stone travelled down an inclined plane to the wharf. If you look behind the canalside house opposite, you will see masonry sloping uphill, indicating the course of the plane, which is now an access road. It was built in 1803 with wooden rails, but was realigned and fitted with cast-iron rails around 1826. It was still operating over 30 years later, for, when the lease of Murhill Quarries was advertised in the *Bath Chronicle* on 2 April 1857, it included 'five labourers' cottages, a large wharf and landing crane on the bank of the Kennet and Avon Canal, two cranes in the quarry, steam engine for sawing up stone, chains, truck, trollies and railway, with an inclined plane for delivering the stone on the wharf'.

In 1898, Murhill was the site of a spectacular breach in the canal bank. On 3 March 1898, the *Bath Chronicle* reported that

> the bank of the Kennet and Avon Canal ... collapsed on Monday morning at Murhill, a few miles above Bath. A vast volume of water escaped through the gap, which was twelve yards wide, flooding the low-lying pastures adjacent. The water eventually made its way into the Avon, which was greatly swollen. Fortunately there was no navigation going on, but two men working on a punt had a narrow escape. They left the punt only a minute before the slip occurred, and saw their punt and tools swept away at an enormous velocity. Dams were soon erected, but some hundreds of pounds of damage was done.

A salutary reminder that the tranquillity of this stretch of the canal relies on the constant maintenance of a prodigious piece of civil engineering.

After passing Bridge 174, you will see a bridge carrying the railway across the Avon. Just beyond it, the River Frome flows into the Avon, and, although the bridge hides the point where the two rivers meet, it does not hide the glorious view up the Frome valley. Shortly after this, the canal curves to run alongside the railway. The large building you can

---

1 See *Bath Chronicle*, 24 December 1846

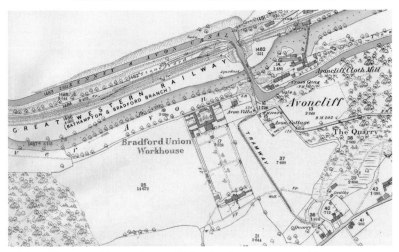

A late 19th-century OS map of Avoncliff, showing the workhouse and the quarry tramway which crossed the aqueduct to a stone yard next to the railway

A postcard of the workhouse after its conversion to a war hospital. The course of the inclined plane can be seen on the left.

see across the river was built around 1795 to accommodate workers in the nearby mills, but in 1835 was converted to a workhouse. In 1917 it became a war hospital, six years later it became a hotel, but in the Second World War it was requisitioned to provide offices for the British Museum, many of whose treasures were stored in underground quarries nearby. It has now been converted into a row of twelve houses called Ancliff Square. High on the hillside behind it is Greenhill House, built in the mid-18th century but extended in the early 20th.

Two early 20th-century postcards of Avoncliff Aqueduct, looking south (above) and north (below), with the rails of the tramway still in place

After passing another stop gate, the canal curves right to cross Avoncliff Aqueduct. A tramway once ran along the towpath here, carrying stone which came down an inclined plane from Westwood Quarry, high in the hillside ahead, to a stone yard alongside the railway.

After crossing Avoncliff Aqueduct, bear right and go down steps to a subway under the canal. From here, you can see how the central arch of the aqueduct has sagged. This happened shortly after it was built, possibly because inferior stone from the quarry at Conkwell was used to build it (see pages 128-9). The subway leads to the Cross Guns, which, as the first pub since Bath, may well be a tempting prospect.

⇄ *If you want to head back from here, walk along the path on the east side of the aqueduct and go down steps to Avoncliff station, from where trains run roughly every hour to Bath.*

To continue on to Bradford on Avon, follow the towpath round the back of the Cross Guns, and look for a path on the left leading into Barton Farm Country Park (ST806600). *Follow it as it zigzags down to the river and bear right through a broad meadow* with occasional glimpses of the river through the undergrowth. After going through a gate and crossing a footbridge, you pass a labyrinth made of willow.

The river at Avoncliff

After going through another gate, continue along a gravel path, which eventually joins a tarmac path. The outskirts of Bradford on Avon are now only minutes away, and there is no finer approach to one of England's most historic towns, for your first view of it is one that has not changed, in its essentials, for over 600 years. Through the trees, you can glimpse the arches of Barton Bridge, built in the 14th century, and just wide enough to accommodate a packhorse. *Then, as the path curves, Bradford's monumental tithe barn comes into view.* It too dates from the 14th century, when this busy little town was one of the jewels in the crown of Shaftesbury Abbey, the second richest nunnery in all England. Bradford was already a well-established town with a 300-year-old monastery when King Aethelred II gave it to the abbey in AD1001. The size and magnificence of the tithe barn stands testament to the town's wealth in the middle ages, which came largely

The tithe barn c1900

from the weaving trade. The barn stood within the curtilage of a grange or farm run by the abbey. The two buildings to the north of it are also 14th century, while Barton Farmhouse, beyond them, although rebuilt in the 18th century, incorporates some of the medieval grange.

From here, you could carry on along the river, and, after going under the railway, turn right to the station. It would be a pity, however, to leave Bradford on Avon without a quick look at some of its other treasures, and, although mindful that you have already walked over nine miles, there is a short detour that is just about unmissable.[1] It also has the advantage of ending in the middle of town, where there is an excellent choice of pubs and cafes.

It starts by heading across a footbridge to a small island with a World War II pillbox (see page 148) *before continuing across Barton Bridge. On the far side, where there is a choice of paths, take the one on the right. Go through a gate, cross the railway and head up steps to another gate. Continue up a path between walls, which swings right past a gazebo. A little further along, bear left up steps* to emerge opposite a pair of 17th-century cottages with a passageway running through them to another cottage at the back. This street, known as Newtown , dates from the late 17th century, when, after the revival of the clothing trade following the arrival of Flemish weavers – and Flemish weaving practices – to the town, its population increased rapidly.

As you ***bear right***, you pass the site of brewery buildings once attached to the old Seven Stars Inn further along. Between 1859 and 1864, the Wilkins family, who owned the Seven Stars, embarked on

1 For more information on the town, see Fassnidge, *Bradford on Avon: Past and Present.*

a major expansion programme, building the massive new brewery which you can see ahead. Initially known as the Seven Stars Brewery, it was renamed the Newtown Brewery, and later the Pickwick Brewery, before being acquired by Usher's of Trowbridge in 1920. Although Usher's closed the brewery and demolished some of the older buildings adjoining the Seven Stars, the main brewery building survived, being used by various companies until it was converted to offices and flats in 1991. The inn also survived until last orders were finally called in 1969.

Head past the archway – with seven stars emblazoned above it – and turn up a ramp, looking out for caves hollowed out of the rock

as you climb past the brewery. Just before the path forks at a metal post, bear left up a narrow flight of steps which leads to a range of terraces, mostly dating from around 1800, called the Tory. The name, in case you are wondering, has no political connotation; it comes from the word 'tor', meaning 'hill'. *Bear left past Mountain Cottage and Tory House, and go through a gateway to the Chapel of St Mary Tory*, where a holy spring flows from the hillside. From here there are spectacular views over the town and southwards to the White Horse at Westbury. By the mid-19th century, the original medieval chapel had virtually crumbled away. Only a fragment of the east wall remained, and what you see today is a Victorian reconstruction.

View over Bradford on Avon from the Tory

Retrace your steps and carry on along the Tory, with views down to some of the mills on which the town's prosperity once rested. *When you reach Nº 10, turn right down steps to a row of 17th and 18th century cottages called Middle Rank, and turn left. Follow the path as it heads down to emerge on Newtown.* Looking left, the long building you can see along the street dates from around 1470 and was originally a barn attached to a medieval manor house that stood behind it. The building on your right, with a datestone of 1695, is the old Bell Inn. Although it closed in 1965, the bracket from which a large bell once hung can still be seen.

Turn right along Newtown, passing more 17th century buildings – including two with 1697 datestones – and another lost inn, the Masons Arms, closed in 2005 but still with its faded sign. The Ropewalk complex on your left occupies the site of a school demolished in 1984, which once had a ropewalk in front of it. At Nº 39 is yet another lost pub, the White Lion, which closed around 150 years ago but still has a ghost sign for HOME BREWED BEERS.

Just before a lopsided two-storey cottage tacked onto the end of a larger building, turn left down steps. To your right, at the bottom of the steps, is Barton Orchard. What appears to be a row of four-storey 18th-century houses is in fact a row of two-storey weavers' cottages entered from the front, with another row of two-storey cottages, entered from the back, above. Facing you is the Chantry, dating from the mid-16th century, but greatly altered. At one time it was owned by clothiers who built a factory (since demolished) adjoining it. It has also been a school and is now divided into two private houses – the Chantry and Little Chantry.

Carry on down a path beside the Chantry, and, at the churchyard gates, turn to look back at the imposing east front of Little Chantry, added in the 18th century. As you *carry on past Holy Trinity church*, look out for Orpin's House on the left. This was the home of Edward Orpin, immortalised in a painting, formerly attributed to Gainsborough, called *The Parish Clerk*.

A little further on, at the end of a row of cottages, you come to the most remarkable building in a

St Lawrence's church, 1887

town of remarkable buildings. St Lawrence's church was probably built around AD1000, using ashlar stone from Hazelbury (see page 204). After Holy Trinity was built across the road in the 12th century, it was converted to an ossuary, where the bones of the dead were stored. Later, it became a cloth factory, but, by the 19th century, hemmed in by a variety of other buildings – including some right up against its walls – the nave, with an extra floor inserted, had become a school, while the chancel was a cottage. Then, in the mid-1850s, detective work by a local clergyman established its true provenance. Restoration got under way a few years later, and today, stripped of later accretions and with the buildings that hid it long gone, it stands forth in its ancient glory.

Although just about anything would be an anticlimax after St Lawrence's, there is plenty more to see as you carry on. First comes the uncompromising bulk of Abbey Mills. Its five storeys have towered over Church Street since 1875, when it was built as a clothing mill. It later became a rubber factory, but has now been converted to retirement flats. Abbey House, behind the wall on the left, was built around 1775, but incorporates a much older building. Opposite its entrance gates is Dutch Barton, 17th century but refronted, on its east side, in the 18th century. The road beside it leads up to Druce's Hill House, built in the 1730s, with some 17th-century gabled houses to the left. Opposite Dutch Barton is a 16th-century church house, now a Masonic Hall. The walled garden beyond it stands on the site of the Ship Inn, which, after changing its name to the Carpenter's Arms, closed in the 1880s and was demolished in 1922.

Next door, set well back, is Church House, built around 1730 and once a bank. Then, at the end of the street, a massive oriel window and broad Jacobean-style gables lead to an elaborate pepperpot tower set diagonally on the corner, and dominating the scene. Now a Roman Catholic church, it was built in 1854 as Bradford's town hall by Thomas Fuller of Bath, who, after emigrating to Canada, designed the parliament buildings in Ottawa.

Opposite is the Swan Hotel, dating from 1500 but rebuilt in the 18th century. The building to the right of it was, as a plaque records, once the Red Lion. *Cross at the zebra crossing and bear right downhill to the Shambles*, from where you can look across to a magnificent if sadly faded sign painted around 1902 on the side wall of the Swan.

You are now in the heart of Bradford on Avon, where there is a wide choice of bars, pubs and cafés. *To get to the station, carry on along the road, turn right at the mini roundabout and cross the bridge, famous for the 17th-century lock-up halfway across. Carry on along the main road, and at the next mini-roundabout, turn right into Station Place.* 🚉

The Riddle of the Stones

The standing stones at the southern end of Bushey Norwood have long been the source of speculation and conjecture, and in the age of the internet it is only to be expected that theories as to their origin should have proliferated. Many of those theories, not surprisingly, have focused on the possibility that they once formed part of a stone circle or avenue. Although there is a more prosaic theory as to their origin – that they were marker stones for a racecourse that existed hereabouts in the 18th century – this is by no means certain, and has been contested on the grounds that the racecourse was further to the west, a claim which seems to be borne out by Thorpe's map of 1742.

It was to try to get to the bottom of the mystery that I decided to set about discovering what, if anything, antiquarians and writers from earlier centuries had had to say about the stones. From the outset, I realised that my chances of solving the riddle of the stones were slim. What I did not anticipate was how much of a Pandora's Box I would be prising open. Far from settling the matter of the stones on Bushey Norwood, every fresh discovery seemed to reveal another site where traces of a stone circle or avenue had been identified.

So my initial – and rather modest – quest, to shed light on the Bushey Norwood stones, was transformed into something more far-reaching and more fascinating – the record of successive attempts to interpret or impose meaning on the chaotic ruins of the distant past.

The story starts in 1822, when that indefatigable and highly-regarded amateur archaeologist John Skinner, rector of Camerton, made a detailed survey of Bathampton Down. On the map he sketched of the down, what he described as 'large stones lying on the surface' are shown at the western end of the down, some 300-400m east of Sham Castle. He also made a sketch of three of the stones – nine, six and a half, and four feet long respectively – which he described as 'stones near the western Fosse on Hampton Down apparently dug out and used in some religious circle or British work'.[1]

Skinner's conjecture seems to have been forgotten, but 34 years later, when the British Archaeological Association met in Bath, they were presented with evidence of other possible circles. The Rev HM Scarth,

1 British Museum MS 33671 (reproduced in Thomas & Oswin, *The Search for Bathampton Down Stone Circles*, p 9)

a noted local antiquarian, presented a paper on 'the ancient British and Belgic settlement on Hampton Down'. After describing the site, he went on to claim that

> the most curious and important feature of this camp ... seems to have been unnoticed when it was surveyed by Mr Skinner ... and that is the two enclosures on the sloping side of the hill towards the river (not far from the track-way on the north-east which led into the camp), and which are approached by avenues of stones. In two of these enclosures are the remains of stone circles similar in appearance to those of Stanton Drew; unhappily the larger stones have been removed within the memory of some of the present generation, in order to construct fancy cromlechs in the park, or to form rock-work for gardens! The smaller stones now only remain, and how much their original order may have been disarranged by the removal of the larger, we cannot tell, for about 30 have been taken away. This is much to be regretted, as such a vestige of the religious or civil habits of the primaeval inhabitants of this land cannot now be replaced.[1]

He also took members of the association on a guided walk across Bathampton Down, and, 'in traversing what was formerly the stone avenue leading to the temple, or site of judicial assemblies, Mr Scarth expressed regret that the only few remains should be carried away to form ornaments in gardens, and stated that it was only a fortnight previous that a wagon was on the down carrying away the stones'.[2]

A map, based on the Rev Scarth's findings, and described as a 'plan of the remains of the Belgic Camp and Temple at Hampton Down, near Bath' was prepared by Spackman & Sons, surveyors of Bath.[3] This showed the 'remains of the temple' at the eastern end of the camp. Although the area where Skinner had seen large stones lying on the surface is included in the map, no mention is made of them, possibly because they had by carried away by this time.

Up to this time, little attention had been paid to Bushey Norwood, which lay beyond the southern ramparts of the camp, and no one had mentioned the existence of any standing stones there. In 1874, however, Henry Duncan Skrine, who already owned Warleigh Manor, bought Claverton Manor, which included Bushey Norwood. He was a keen amateur antiquarian and archaeologist, and in a talk to Bath's Literary & Philosophical Association in 1888, described how his interest in Bushey Norwood's prehistory was first awakened:

---

1 *Bath Chronicle*, 4 September 1856; Scarth's description of ruined stone circles similar to those at Stanton Drew recalls Tunstall's description of ruined stone circles on Charmy Down in the 1840s (see page 113).

2 *Gentleman's Magazine*, 1856

3 Reproduced in Macdonald, 'Bathampton Down'

Riding one day over this field, I had observed some banks similar to those I had seen on the Hampton Down; and in one place I saw what looked like a foundation of a wall cropping up above the green sward. I set some men digging, and very soon we found my conjecture was right; and following this up we have exposed the foundations of an irregular building of an oval shape, the wall being three feet high, and from six to eight feet in thickness, and inclosing an area of 89 feet by 60. We are now trenching it over, and have found numerous fragments of pottery, and some stone implements, fragments of querns, and flakes of flint, teeth, and bones of domestic animals, and a quantity of burnt stones. Closely adjoining this building are considerable banks, also inclosing areas of various size; some of these probably being arable fields, but the one close to the building on the east appears to have been fortified.

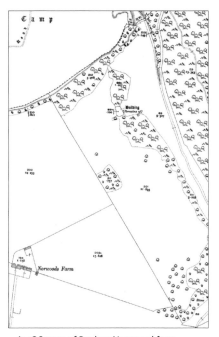

An OS map of Bushey Norwood from around 1905, showing not only the remains of the building discovered by Skrine, but also a stone at the southern end of the field

The whole of these inclosures are connected with the Camp by a ridge running up to what was the original ditch of the Camp on the south side. The inclosure now under examination resembles both in shape and dimensions an undoubted ancient British tribal dwelling which I saw in Cornwall last winter, at a place called Chy-oster, near Penzance.'[1]

Skrine's observations, which seem both meticulous and plausible, failed to include any reference to standing stones. Forty years later, however, the institution was addressed by Gerald Grey, who gave a somewhat more elaborate account of Skrine's discoveries. 'Many years ago,' he informed them,

the late Mr Duncan Skrine, then Squire of Claverton Manor, discovered an early British dwelling, and traces of a miniature stone avenue. Mr

1 *Bath Chronicle*, 27 December 1888

Skrine had the site uncovered for inspection by the British Association who then visited Bath. It was not improbable that might have been the site of a small Sun Temple, and the early British settlement in Bushy [sic] Norwood was occupied by the Druid priest or headman, who attended to the rites of the Temple. Many of the stones had been removed to form rockeries, some being in the Clifton Zoo grounds. The stone avenue led to a rough square enclosure, where probably the early British inhabitants erected a wooden palisade for defence.[1]

Where the information concerning the stone avenue came from is unclear, but it quickly became accepted fact. Two years later, for example, the *Chonicle's* 'Weekly Ramble' guided readers to Bushey Norwood, informing them that 'from this sequestered corner of the down came the stones with which the Botanic Garden's famous rockeries were fashioned, and here many remain in two well-defined lines leading to the hut-dwelling.'[2]

Skrine's discoveries were towards the northern end of Bushey Norwood, some distance away from the standing stones, so, even if there had been a stone avenue, they would not have formed part of it. With the waters now well and truly muddied, and the stones well on their way to be accepted – in the popular imagination at least – as the remains of an Avebury-like avenue – a correspondent in the *Bath Chronicle* – identified only as 'ATW of Monkton Combe' asked if anyone could clear the matter up:

> In the field called Bushey Norwood, on Claverton Down, is an upright stone with a hole in it. As this has been and may be again taken for a holed stone of prehistoric origin ... it may be well to know its origin. The hole in the stone is obviously due to the limestone weathering when the stone was recumbent upon its bed. I have heard two accounts of its origin, firstly that it was erected to commemorate the fatal duel between Viscount du Barri and Count de Rice, and more prosaically that it commemorates a favourite horse. Can anyone give accurate information upon this point?[3]

If ATW thought this would settle the question of the stones, he could not have been more wrong. Gerald Grey was first to reply:

> I know the stone of old. There were many like it when first I knew Bushey Norwood. The late squire, Mr Henry Duncan Skrine, had this particular stone raised upright to mark the spot where he had one or two favourite horses buried. The rest of the stones were used in the Bath Botanical Gardens and the Clifton Zoo for making rockeries. The site of the Du Barri duel was on the boundary of Claverton and

---

1 *Bath Chronicle*, 21 January 1928
2 *Bath Chronicle*, 25 January 1930
3 *Bath Chronicle*, 1 July 1933

THE RIDDLE OF THE STONES

Bathampton Downs. A rough stone against the wall marks the spot where Du Barri lay all day before he was removed to Bathampton for the inquest and burial.[1]

So far so good, and there the matter might have rested, had not another reader – 'KES' of Exmouth – been moved to reply the following week:

> So far, the response to the enquiry of ATW for exact information concerning the holed stone in Bushy Norwood, has been far from exact, and fails to touch the significance that really attaches to the stone. Its upright position is immaterial, and may have served some comparatively modern pastoral purpose; but it was so standing in the boyhood of old inhabitants of Claverton Down, and inquiries made by me some years ago failed to confirm the report that it marked the grave of Mr HD Skrine's favourite horses. Members of the Skrine family knew nothing about it.
>
> The importance of the stone lies in the fact that it is one of a great number that once formed a stone avenue up to the summit of Hampton Down, before ever the 'Camp' there existed. Everything that has been written by Prebendary Scarth about the stone circles and avenues on the north side of Hampton Camp, pointing to the existence of a Temple of the Sun there, centuries before the Roman occupation, applies to the vestiges which still remain in Bushy Norwood on the south. Numbers of the stones lie cast down, still sufficiently in situ to indicate an avenue, but most of them were removed at different periods to the grounds of Claverton Manor, where some of them may be seen as rock-work, and some set upright in the farm-drive to the back of the manor – probably marking the graves of favourite animals ...
>
> From the early ages Bushy Norwood has never been under agricultural cultivation, and the numerous antiquities that are there were first discovered in 1887 by Mr HD Skrine ... Prebendary Scarth had apparently no knowledge of the antiquities hidden by the bushes of this field; but the stone avenue had been noticed by the Rev John Skinner, of Camerton, and is mentioned in his MS writings ...
>
> The stones given by Mr HD Skrine for the Bath Botanical Gardens did not come from Bushy Norwood, but from the northern slope of Hampton Down, whereby the Druidical remains noticed by Prebendary Scarth were wrecked. These had, however, been charted for him on a huge map, which still exists in the office of Mr Keith W Calvert.
>
> About the stones taken to the Clifton Zoo I know nothing; but years ago a great circle of stones in Bushy Norwood were uncovered for a visit of the British Association from Bristol, and were subsequently removed – only the holes remaining. Perhaps it was to Clifton that they went, for they were not taken into the grounds of Claverton Manor.
>
> The stones referred to are all great slabs of the layer of rock that lies above the oolite formation, and holes in them are frequently found caused by the action of water or of tree roots as the rock was forming. The Druids would have found them to hand in abundance for their

temples and avenues. According to Wood the Elder, Ralph Allen's roads were made of the smashed atoms of a Druid's Temple that was destroyed in the building of Prior Park mansion.[1]

This prompted the original correspondent, ATW, to weigh back in:

The reply of KES raises a number of points outside my original query. My query was an endeavour to find out when and why the stone was raised. That it was raised at no distant date is, I believe, proved by the relatively small amount of weathering on what was the underside. It may or may not have been raised in memory of a horse. It is in fact improbable that a horse was buried at the stone itself because there is practically no soil covering the rock at that point.

The second point is the statement that the stone was one of an avenue of stones leading to Bathampton Down. In support of this it is said that the stone avenue had been noticed by the Rev John Skinner, of Camerton. I have a very considerable acquaintance with Mr Skinner's Journals. He paid many visits to Bathampton Down ... In spite of his habit of continually repeating the same information in different contexts, I cannot recall any reference to this avenue. I think that if there had been an avenue of stones here, so near to Bath ... it would not have escaped notice all these years.

The next point is the significance of the stones that used to be visible on the north slope of Bathampton Down. I have seen the large scale plan in Mr Calvert's office. It is, I believe, the original of the plan in Mr Skrine's pamphlet ... No coherent plan could be detected in the stones as depicted. Had they former a prehistoric monument of importance, it is most unlikely that they would have been missed by the indefatigable Stukeley in the 18th century, or by the careful antiquary Aubrey, who noted other remains in the Bath district a century earlier.[2]

To which names could be added that of the architect John Wood, who was obsessed with stone circles, made detailed surveys of Stonehenge and Stanton Drew, and based the design and dimensions of the Circus in Bath on Stonehenge. He knew the area around Bath intimately and wrote about its antiquities at great length. Of Bathampton Down, he wrote that 'it shews the Footsteps of a infinite Number of Stone Walls'. If he had suspected that any of those stones once formed part of an avenue or circle, there is no question but that he would have investigated further.

That is not the end of the story, however. In 1958, Professor EK Tratman of the University of Bristol examined Scarth's claims as part of his research into the lost stone circles of North Somerset.[3] Examining Spackman's map, he calculated that the grid reference of the site

1 *Bath Chronicle*, 12 August 1933
2 *Bath Chronicle*, 19 August 1933
3 Tratman, 'The Lost Stone Circles of North Somerset'

identified by Scarth was ST772652. He also concluded that, despite Scarth having relied heavily on anecdotal evidence – 'the memory of some of the present generation' – there seemed 'no reason to doubt Scarth's explicit statement that the circles and avenues were there'.

Then, in 2010-11, after a dowser called Paul Daw visited the site and produced a plan of two stone circles whose sites he claimed to have discovered, members of the Bath & Camerton Archaeological Society carried out a geophysical survey, and concluded that that they were 'cautiously optimistic that there was a hilltop stone circle here'.

So, despite nobody having spotted it until Scarth detected its vestigial profile, it seems as though there may have been a stone circle on Bathampton Down after all. However, as there is nothing to see above ground, and the site is not only on private land but also home to nesting skylarks, it should not be visited without prior permission.

As for the stones on Bushey Norwood, the riddle seems more intractable than ever. The problem with the theory that they were connected with the racecourse – leaving aside the racecourse's precise location – is that they do not look like the sort of stones that would be have been used as markers. They do, on the other hand, look very much like the sort of stones found in Neolithic circles and avenues. But it is odd that Mr Skrine seems to have made no mention of them, odd too that his family were unable to help 'KES' with his enquiries. Perhaps they chose not to share whatever information they had with him. Perhaps Skrine, with his interest in the distant past, had raised a few stones, as landowners did elsewhere, as a sort of Druidic folly, and, its genesis having been forgotten, his family were content to let the secret rest. One thing is certain. The riddle of the stones is one that will continue to intrigue those who walk through this glorious meadow high above the Avon valley.

Bibliography

'Assessment of archaeological resource in aggregate-producing areas of Bath & North East Somerset', English Heritage Project No 5850, Museum of London Archaeology, in association with Bath & North East Somerset Council, April 2013 (The report can be downloaded at archaeologydataservice.ac.uk/archives/view/banes_eh_2014)

Allsop, Niall, *The Somersetshire Coal Canal Rediscovered: A Walker's Guide* (revised edition), Bath, 1993

Atthill, Robin, *The Somerset & Dorset Railway*, Newton Abbot, 1967

Baddeley, MJB, *Bath and Bristol and Forty Miles Around*, London, 1902

Bodman, Martin, *Inclined Planes in the South West*, Truro, 2012

Buchanan, Brenda, 'Bath's Forgotten Gunpowder History: The Powder Mills at Woolley in the Eighteenth Century', in *Bath History*, x, 72-96

Castens, Simon, *On the Trail of The Titfield Thunderbolt*, Limpley Stoke, 2000

Clew, Kenneth R, *The Somersetshire Coal Canal & Railways*, Newton Abbot, 1970

Collinson, Rev John, *The History and Antiquities of the County of Somerset* (3 vols), 1791 (reprinted Gloucester, 1983)

Davenport, Peter, '"The Belgic Camp and Temple" Map', in *The Survey of Bath & District: Newsletter of the Survey of Old Bath and Its Associates*, 4, November 1995, p 23

Dobbie, Beatrice Willmott, *Batheaston: An English Rural Community*, Bath, 1969

Dodge, Alan, *Freshford: The History of a Somerset Village*, Freshford, 2000

Down, CG & AJ Warrington, *The History of the Somerset Coalfield*, Newton Abbot, 1971

Egan, Pierce, *Walks through Bath*, Bath, 1819

Elliott, Kirsten, *Foul Deeds & Suspicious Deaths in Bath*, Barnsley, 2007

Elliott, Kirsten, *Queen of Waters: A Journey in Time along the Kennet & Avon Canal*, Bath, 2012

Eyles, JM, 'William Smith's Home Near Bath: The Real Tucking Mill', *Journal of the Society for the Bibliography of Natural History*, 7, 1974, 29-34

Fassnidge, Harold, *Bradford on Avon: Past and Present* (expanded edition), Bradford on Avon, 1993

Fawcett, Trevor, *Bath Entertain'd*, Bath, 1998

Fosker, Oliver, *The Titfield Thunderbolt: Now & Then*, Woodbridge, Suffolk, 2008

Foyle, Andrew & Nikolaus Pevsner, *The Buildings of England: Somerset: North and Bristol*, New Haven & London, 2011

Hawkins, Derek, *Subterranean Britain: Bath Stone Quarries*, Monkton Farleigh, 2011

Hobbs, PRN & GO Jenkins, *Bath's 'foundered strata' – a re-interpretation*, British Geological Survey, 2008 (nora.nerc.ac.uk/14771/1/OR08052.pdf)

Ibbetson, Laporte & J Hassell, *A Picturesque Guide to Bath, Bristol-Hotwells, The River Avon, and the Adjacent Country*, London, 1793

Kerr, John, *Sydney Gardens Vauxhall, Bath: Syllabus or Descriptive Representations of the Numerous Productions of Nature and Art Presented in this Extensive Establishment*, Bath, 1825

La Trobe-Bateman, Emily & Rosalind Niblett, *Bath: An Archaeological Assessment*, Oxford & Philadelphia, 2016

Leech, Roger, *Small Medieval Towns in Avon: Archaeology and Planning*, Cheltenham, 1975

Macdonald, John, 'Bathampton Down', in *The Survey of Bath & District: Newsletter of the Survey of Old Bath and Its Associates*, 4, November 1995, pp. 21-2 (historyofbath.org.uk/Publications/Survey of Old Bath 04.pdf)

Macmillen, Neil & Mike Chapman, *Coal from Camerton* (revised & enlarged), Lydney, 2014

Maggs, Colin & Gerry Beale, *The Camerton Branch*, Upper Bucklebury, Berks, 1985

Major, Albany F & Edward J Burrow, *The Mystery of Wansdyke*, Cheltenham, 1926

Manco, Jean, *The Parish of Englishcombe: A History*, Englishcombe, 1995 (www.englishcombe.net/pdf/englishcombe history - manco.pdf)

Mee, Arthur, *The King's England: Somerset*, London, 1940

Mowl, Tim & Brian Earnshaw, *John Wood: Architect of Obsession*, Bath, 1988

Oswin, John & Rick Buettner, *Little Solsbury Hill Camp: Geophysical Survey, Bath & Camerton Archaeological Society, 2012*, Bath, 2014 (www.bacas.org.uk/Reports/Solsbury%20Report%20web%20final_.pdf)

Pevsner, Nikolaus (rev. Bridget Cherry), *The Buildings of England: Wiltshire*, Harmondsworth, 1975

Pollard, David, 'Bath stone quarry railways 1795-1830' in *Bristol Industrial Archaeological Society Journal*, 15, 1982, pp. 13-19

Quinn, Phil, *Holy Wells of the Bath & Bristol Region*, Almeley, 1999

Rack, Edmund, *Survey of Somerset*, edited by Mark McDermott & Sue Berry, Taunton, 2011

Sloman, Susan, *Gainsborough in Bath*, New Haven & London, 2002

Thicknesse, Philip, *The New Prose Bath Guide*, London, 1778

Thomas, Rod, *A Sacred Landscape: The Prehistory of Bathampton Down*, Bath, 2008

Thomas, Rod & John Oswin, 'Bathampton Down Stone Circles', in *Camertonia: Journal of the Bath & Camerton Archaeological Society*, 50, 2012, pp. 14-16 (www.bacas.org.uk/archive/articles/99)

Thomas, Rod & John Oswin, *The Search for Bathampton Down Stone Circles*, Bath & Camerton Archaeological Society (www.bacas.org. uk/Reports/BathamptonDown1-3screen.pdf)

Tratman EK, 'The Lost Stone Circles of North Somerset', in *Proceedings of the University of Bristol Spelaeological Association*, 8, 110-18 (www. ubss.org.uk/resources/proceedings/vol8/UBSS_Proc_8_2_110-118.pdf)

Tunstall, James, *Rambles about Bath and its Neighbourhood*, London & Bath (2nd edition), 1848

Tunstall, James & REM Peach, *Rambles about Bath and its Neighbourhood, based on Dr Tunstall's Work*, London & Bath, 1889

Warner, Rev Richard, *Excursions from Bath*, Bath & London, 1801

Wheatcroft, Mrs L, *Picturesque Village Rambles round Bath*, reprinted from *The Bath & County Graphic*, Oct 1896-June 1898, Bath

Wood, John, *An Essay towards a Description of Bath* (2 vols), London, 1749

Wroughton, John, *The Battle of Lansdown, 1643: An Explorer's Guide*, Bath, 2008

In adddition to published sources, I have consulted numerous online resources, many of which are cited in the footnotes. Several of the more recondite articles in academic journals and other publications, listed in the bibliography, can also be found online, and, where relevant, this is indicated. Four other websites deserve special mention: the British Newspaper Archive (www.britishnewspaperarchive.co.uk), which includes a seachable online archive of the *Bath Chronicle*, along with many other newspapers; the Internet Archive (archive.org), which includes searchable online texts of many rare books, such as John Wood's *Description of Bath*, Tunstall's *Rambles about Bath*, and Egan's *Walks through Bath*; and two websites which include a selection of historic maps – Know Your Place (maps.bristol.gov.uk/kyp/?edition=banes) and the National Library of Scotland (maps.nls.uk/geo/explore/).

Acknowledgements & Picture Credits

First and foremost, thanks go to my wife, Kirsten Elliott, who not only accompanied me on many of the walks, but also helped with research and undertook the task of proof reading.

Thanks also to Colin Johnston and the staff of Bath Record Office for permission to reproduce many of the old maps, especially Thomas Thorpe's 1742 'Survey of the City of Bath ... and of Five Miles Round'.

Shorter versions of some of the walks have appeared in *The Bath Magazine*, and I am grateful to the editor, Georgette McCready, for permission to reproduce them here.

Thanks also to Geoff Hiscocks for the photograph on page 26; Simon Castens for that on page 138; Geoff Alford and Simon Castens for that on page 180; and Paul De'Ath for that at the top of page 215. All other photographs are from the Akeman Press Archive.

More books from Akeman Press

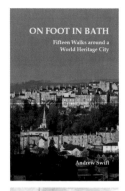

On Foot in Bath
Andrew Swift
Fifteen walks around Bath, ranging from
gentle strolls through the city's streets
to country walks which visit spectacular
buildings high in the surrounding hills.
£15

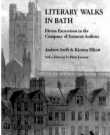

Literary Walks in Bath
Andrew Swift & Kirsten Elliott
Bath seen through the eyes of Charles
Dickens, Tobias Smollett, John Betjeman,
Mary Shelley, Fanny Burney, Jane Austen,
Tom Paine, Georgette Heyer and many
others.
£15

Ghost Signs of Bath
Andrew Swift & Kirsten Elliott
Nowhere are ghost signs advertising
long-defunct businesses found in greater
abundance or variety than on the streets
of Bath. This book tells the story behind
over 160 ghost signs in Bath and the
surrounding area.
£16.99

Queen of Waters
Kirsten Elliott
This classic account of the
Kennet & Avon Canal includes
chapters on the Somersetshire
Coal Canal, the Wilts & Berks
Canal and the Avon Navigation.
£20

Available from bookshops or direct (with free postage in the UK) from Akeman Press

More books from Akeman Press

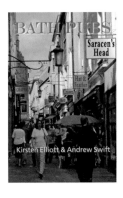

Bath Pubs
Kirsten Elliott & Andrew Swift
First published in 2003, this classic account
told the history of all of Bath's surviving
pubs. Many have since closed, lending an
added poignancy to their stories, and an
increased appreciation of those that remain.
£12.99

Awash with Ale: 2000 Years of Imbibing in Bath
Andrew Swift & Kirsten Elliott
The story of Bath's long love affair with
the demon drink, from the gin craze to
the beerhouse boom, and from the cider
rebellion to the Drunken Election.
£12.99

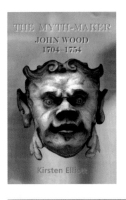

The Mythmaker: John Wood
Kirsten Elliott
The astonishing story of how Druidic
myths, mysticism and alchemy inspired
Bath's most celebrated architect to create
some of the city's most iconic buildings.
£10

Bath City Paintings
Nick Cudworth
A selection of Nick Cudworth's
dramatic views of Bath, chosen
from works painted between 1996
and 2014, each accompanied by a
detailed description by the artist.
£35

More books from Akeman Press

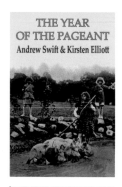

The Year of the Pageant
Andrew Swift & Kirsten Elliott
Rumours of war, rising unemployment, strikes and suffragette rallies – Bath in 1909 was a city in turmoil – yet this was the year in which it mounted a pageant with a cast of thousands to mark its emergence as a heritage tourist destination.
£15

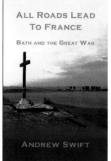

All Roads Lead to France: Bath and the Great War
Andrew Swift
Interweaving letters from soldiers on the front line with stories of life on the home front, this comprehensive account creates a vivid picture of the Great War's impact on the city of Bath.
£15

Somerset Follies
Jonathan Holt
A fascinating guide to Somerset's most bizarre and eccentric buildings, including over 25 in and around Bath.
£10

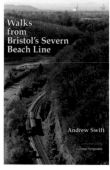

Walks from Bristol's Severn Beach Line
Andrew Swift
Sixteen walks from stations on the Severn Beach Line, ranging from short strolls along Georgian crescents and tree-lined parades to walks through ancient woodlands, 18th-century estates and spectacular river gorges.
£15

Available from bookshops or direct (with free postage in the UK) from Akeman Press

More books from Akeman Press

Childhood Memories
Pauline Forrest
A classic account of working-class life in the Avon Street area of Bath and Weston village in the 1920s and 1930s. Illustrated with never before published archive photographs and paintings.
£6.50

The Ringing Grooves of Change
Andrew Swift
The epic story of how Isambard Kingdom Brunel – and an army of navvies – built the railway through Bath, changing the face of the city forever.
£12

Devon Pubs
Andrew Swift & Kirsten Elliott
Archive photographs of over 450 historic inns and alehouses, plus chapters on Devon's lost breweries, church house inns, the history of cider making, Devon White Ale and Uncle Tom Cobley and all.
£15

Pieroni's Fountain
Colin Fisher
The story of Stefano Pieroni, one of Victorian Bath's most colourful characters – sculptor, publican, art dealer, volunteer rifleman – and Italian patriot.
£10